CALLED BEFORE BIRTH

CALLED BEFORE BIRTH

THE AUTOBIOGRAPHY OF HELEN LAWRENCE

AuthorHouse™
1663 Liberty Drive
Bloomington, IN 47403
www.authorhouse.com
Phone: 1-800-839-8640

© 2013 by HELEN LAWRENCE. All rights reserved.

No part of this book may be reproduced, stored in a retrieval system, or transmitted by any means without the written permission of the author.

Published by AuthorHouse   01/09/2013

ISBN: 978-1-4772-5133-1 (sc)
ISBN: 978-1-4817-8095-7 (e)

Any people depicted in stock imagery provided by Thinkstock are models, and such images are being used for illustrative purposes only.
Certain stock imagery © Thinkstock.

This book is printed on acid-free paper.

Because of the dynamic nature of the Internet, any web addresses or links contained in this book may have changed since publication and may no longer be valid. The views expressed in this work are solely those of the author and do not necessarily reflect the views of the publisher, and the publisher hereby disclaims any responsibility for them.

CONTENTS

PREFACE ix
DEDICATION xi
ACKNOWLEDGEMENTS xiii

CHAPTER 1 1
   Early Childhood Memories—Actual and Received 1
   A Dysfunctional Family 6
   From riches to near poverty 7

CHAPTER 2 11
   The War Years 11
   War begins to bite 14
   Move to a new home 15
   War Time Animals 19
   Wartime Schooling 21

CHAPTER 3 25
   Discipline and Daily Life 25
   An Interesting Friend 28
   Two misdemeanours and a fishing adventure 29

It missed me!.. 31
I can't take this any longer!.. 32

CHAPTER 4 35
A New Country and a New Life............................. 35
New Clothes.. 37
Rough waters, pleasant islands 38
We Begin our New Life.. 40
One more move... 42

CHAPTER 5 49
A difficult situation 49
Who is this Jesus?... 53

CHAPTER 6 57
Hospital Life.. 57
God speaks into my life... 60
Becoming a member of a Church......................... 67

CHAPTER 7 69
Life with a purpose... 69
Plans to help my Mother 70
Outdoor life... 73
Life as a Christian 75

CHAPTER 8 77
The Healing Home.. 77

CHAPTER 9 91
The Hostel Warden... 91
What does a Hostel Warden do?.......................... 94
Creature Hazards.. 95
African Culture 97

    Drama 98
    When one needs wisdom 101
    Never underestimate what prayer can do. 104

Chapter 10 109
    Back to England 109
    The Passport and the Passage 112

Chapter 11 119
    Theological College 119
    Misdemeanours at College 126

CHAPTER 12 129
    My First Parish 129
    Main Ministry 133
    Two Amusing Occasions 140

CHAPTER 13 145
    Limitation of early ministry 145
    Limitations of a Lady Worker 147
    The still small voice at St. Jude's 152
    Goddaughters 155
    Colleagues while at St. Jude's 157

Chapter 14 161
    1974-1990 161
    The Young People 170
    A serious situation 171

CHAPTER 15 177
    Ordination 177
    Church Family Holidays 178
    Bad Dog—Good Dog 181

Home Made Entertainment	182
Times of Mission	184
How God Spoke in an Awesome Way	187
Health Problems and Retirement	188

CHAPTER 16 191
    Retirement 191
    Relaxation and Ministry 194
    Ordination 195
    A Very Happy Occasion 205

CHAPTER 17 207
    Remaining Years at Frinton 207
    The Unexpected Takes Place 210

PREFACE

"Before I was born the Lord called me; from my birth He has made mention of my name".
(Isaiah 49 verse 1—
New International Version.)

"Before I formed you in the womb I knew you, before you were born I set you apart".
(Jeremiah I verse 5—
New International Version)

Sometimes in life we ask the question, "Why was I born, what am I here for?" The two verses above have been chosen because they express what I believe is true of my own life, and is the reason for the title of this book. Of course, I had no realisation of the reality of this call until many years later. Nevertheless, I firmly believe this is the truth of what God intended for my life. Therefore this book is written in the hope that all who read it will see God's will being worked out in the life of one of His children. How His plans and purposes are brought about in our lives. How in His love and mercy God overcomes the hurts, the failures, and the inadequacies in our lives to His glory, not ours. Further my hope is that those who read these pages will have their faith and hope in our great God enlivened, strengthened and made sure. Also those who have not yet found faith in Christ will come to see Christ is our Lord and Saviour and the One who gives us the hope of Eternity. This is the hope that the Apostle Peter writes about in his first letter and also the writer of the letter to the Hebrew Christians. 1 Peter 1 verse 3 and Hebrews Chapter 11 verse 1.

I have not achieved great things as many as my fellow Christians. Yet what I have done is not because of any goodness in myself, it is because of God's grace in my life and in His mercy He called me.

DEDICATION

This book is dedicated to Winnie Karsten and Peggie Watson who first introduced me to our Lord Jesus Christ.

ACKNOWLEDGEMENTS

There have been so many people down the years who have been a blessing to me. I fear to mention each by name for I am sure to forget someone. Those who have loved me, advised me, remonstrated with me, been a colleague in the ministry, you know who you are. Thank you. I value you and love you all.

My special thanks to Peter and Beryl Pytches for sharing your family with me, and regarding me as a family member.

The Revd. David Lewis who has spent a lot of his time painstakingly proofreading my book.

CHAPTER 1

Early Childhood Memories—Actual and Received

On the 25th of June 1930 a new child was born into the world. My Mother told me I was born in Birmingham. That is all I know of that very early period of my life.

There are a few early memories like running on a beach in Clacton-on-Sea in Essex while on holiday. I trod on a piece of glass and was taken to a first-aid post where my foot was dressed. I was three to four years old at the time. I can remember playing with my brother Austin, 2 years older than me. We enjoyed sitting on the small platform on the front of a beach hut and getting splashed by the water that came up through the slats of the platform as the tide came in. These were the beach huts on the sea wall that runs alongside the Golf Course at Frinton-on-Sea in Essex, locally known as the Walings.

My mother told me of something I did while quite small. Getting out of my bed one night I went into my Mother's bedroom and got myself dressed in one of my Mother's stage dresses (Mother was on the stage, she was a singer and a dancer). I then made up my face (after a fashion!) and sat at the dressing table where I was found by our Nanny. She put me back into my bed just as I was so my Mother could see what I had got up to. Because of what I looked like my Mother called me Lady Jane. I do not remember this incident, my Mother told me about it. I do know that I was called Jane at home until I went to school, and then my own name was used.

Jeanette
my lost sister

Austin (6 yrs)
and Helen (4 yrs)

Nanny Austin, Helen,
Airedale dog

1934 in the garden
at Ealing
Me at 4 years old

Another received memory is that of my mother throwing a bucket of cold water over me. Apparently, I was prone to getting into a temper. Sounds like the "terrible twos" to me!! It would appear I had refused to do what the Nanny asked me to do and in a temper banged my head against the wall. Then came the cold water treatment. I never lost my temper again. I can think of many times in my life when I have been angry on my own behalf and on behalf of others, but not lost control. My eldest brother Rex, ten years older than me, did have a violent temper. I only witnessed it once. I was already an adult and Rex was home on leave from the army. I cannot remember what caused him to lose his temper, but I do remember clearly the fury which caused him to punch his fist into the wall and injure his hand.

My clearest memories of my childhood go back to the mid 1930's. We were living then in a large house in Ealing, London. At that time my Mother was performing on the stage. My Father had a sweet factory. He was one of the many people affected by the 'Slump'; he went bust and lost everything. It was at this time my brother Rex joined the army. He went into Middlesex Regiment. He made out he was older than he was and got in. He remained in the army until the end of the Second World War. I can remember we had two Airedale dogs during the time in Ealing. I wonder if my lifelong love of dogs began then?

There are some happy memories of this time in Ealing. It would appear we were pretty well off, but that was soon to change.

My Father had a full sized billiard table in one room. Under this table was my brother Austin's beautiful electric Hornby train set. We would sit under the table for hours, Austin getting the trains to move from one point to another, while I sat fascinated watching him and the trains. I had a beautiful doll with real hair that I could wash and brush. I really loved that doll. I have no recollection of what happened to it.

In 1936, the year the Queen Mary liner was built and launched, my brother Austin and I were given a beautiful present. It was a cardboard model of the Queen Mary. The superstructure of the ship lifted off and inside the ship was all sorts of small gifts—small toys and games. I have no idea who gave us this magnificent thing. I remember the delight with which we undid the individual gifts inside.

Although it is a little vague I do remember our being given a sort of buttermilk drink each day (it must have been like the yoghurt drinks we have now). I hated this, it tasted so sour! Then each week we were given liquorice root to chew (this was vile!). I cannot stand liquorice now! Just the thought of it makes me feel nauseous! I guess the Nanny must have been into health food!

A Dysfunctional Family

After living in Ealing we seemed to move from one place to another. I became aware (though I did not understand it) that there was something radically wrong. My mother frequently seemed to me to be behaving in a strange way. She had become an alcoholic. I did not understand what was really wrong for some time. My father was always remonstrating with her and there were some awful rows for many years to come.

By this time my eldest brother Rex was posted to China in his army career. It was in China that he contracted polio and spent one year in a hospital, after which he was in India where he received physiotherapy. He recovered, but was left with a slight limp in one leg. Although he remained in the army he was not able to go to the front in the Second World War.

Rex was obviously a clever chap. He spoke Russian and German fluently, self taught. Although he got no recognition for all his years in the army, at the end of the Second World War he was made a Staff Sergeant and was sent to Germany to act as an interpreter at the Nuremburg Trials. As I write this, it is the sixtieth anniversary of the liberation of the prisoners who were left in Auschwitz. Many of the pictures we are seeing on our television screens at the present time, my brother brought home to us and was able to describe to us the horror of what happened in Auschwitz, Belsen and other camps.

From riches to near poverty

I cannot recall where we went from Ealing. I think I was around six or seven years old. I have a vague recollection of living for a while with a family who were very kind to me. My mother told me at one point that my parents let me stay with these people because they wanted to adopt me. The husband was a doctor. Why they did not adopt me I never found out from my mother.

I should point out there was another child after me, a girl, Jeanette. I only saw her once in my father's sweet factory. She had a great likeness to Shirley Temple. That day I saw her she was having a tantrum. She was stamping her feet and throwing something! When I was an older teenager I told my Mother I would like to find her. After all she was my sister. Mother went berserk and forbade me ever to do anything about it. Neither I nor my brothers were ever able to find out what happened to her.

The next place I remember us living in was a village called Great Holland in Essex, not far from Clacton-on-Sea, a well known seaside resort, also only about a mile away from Frinton-on-Sea which strangely enough I retired to, but more about that in another chapter. In Great Holland we lived in a bungalow with a lot of ground, and several outhouses. There were meadows below the garden which flooded each year. Austin and I had great fun wading through the water in our wellington boots. Nearby there were sand pits. This area now belongs to the Essex Wildlife Trust. It is open for people to walk in and explore. At the end of the area a wood has been planted. The Essex Wildlife Trust holds special events each year. There is pond dipping for children. They organise bird watching, evenings to observe moths, as well as observing other wildlife.

In the time we lived there my brother Austin and myself spent many happy hours playing and catching fish in Holland Brook as well as in the sand pits. One of our favourite pastimes was making dens and climbing trees (for which I was severely punished). The bungalow is still there sixty five years later. I now drive past it on my way to a shopping village and supermarket. The surrounding land must have been sold because there is another large bungalow built where the outhouses used to be.

There is a building at the corner of Little Clacton Road and the main road. This used to be a public house where my mother got her alcohol from when we lived in Great Holland. This building is now a dwelling and is supposed to be awaiting plans for redevelopment.

I remember suffering from mumps and mother leaving me in bed, with a sandwich and a cup of milk. "I have to go out on business", she said. A long time later when she returned she was very drunk. I was always very fearful of her in this condition, frightened of what she might do or say.

It was while we were living at Great Holland that the Second World War broke out. It was the 3rd of September 1939. A nine year old child sitting on the back doorstep in the warm autumn sunshine; the wireless was on and I heard the voice of Neville Chamberlain telling the nation, "I regret to tell you, but we are now at war with Germany". How frightened I was, yet not understanding the full implications of this!

CHAPTER 2

The War Years

1939-1945

September 1939 was a lovely warm month so maybe this gave us a false sense of security about the war. We certainly did not envisage it would last as long as it did.

Each day for most of the time we lived in Great Holland I walked to the village school. My brother and I went together until he had to go to Clacton to a higher school.

It was about one mile to the school which stood then in what was known as The Street, now it is Rectory Road. Sadly, it was demolished in the1950s. It was badly damaged by a bomb shortly after 11pm on Tuesday, 21st September 1943. Rusty railings stand there today as the only memorial to this lovely school.

This school was lovely. Because it was small it was possible for us pupils to receive special care from the teachers. I have a good memory of how patient and kind my teacher was to me. She had a great concern because I was so thin, and I was given extra milk to drink. Those were the days when each child at school had 1/3rd of a pint of milk to drink each day in the break time. I was able to read well, but in those days did not spell well, and arithmetic was never my strong point!! The teacher was just so patient. I was a very timid child, probably because of my background. I certainly had little confidence in myself. Not only then, but through the years at home, if I tried to enter a conversation, for instance, I was told to "shut up" as I could not understand—what did I know?

Among first victims of war

Above: The devastation caused in Victoria Road after the explosion of a C-type mine carried aboard a mine-laying Heinkel which crashed in the centre of Clacton just before midnight on April 30, 1940. Orchard House, number 25, the home of Frederick and Dorothy Gill, has completely disappeared.

Below: Many locals attended the funeral of the four German airmen at Burrsville cemetery — children scattering the coffins with bunches of spring flowers.

CLACTON writer DEREK JOHNSON, author of East Anglia at War 1939-1945, looks back on a fateful night that resulted in the first civilian deaths by enemy action in England during the Second World War.

IN England the first civilian casualties to die through enemy action were at Clacton. But the night of the bombing was actually a terrible accident.

On the night of April 30, 1940, a Heinkel IIIH-4, of the 1st Staffel of Kampfgruppe 126, was laying mines around Norfolk and Suffolk. But the air became engulfed in a thick blanket of fog out at sea.

The plane circled Clacton twice and came down low over the recreation ground as though trying to land.

If the pilot had indeed been trying to land his obviously damaged aircraft on that expanse of open ground then something went dramatically wrong with his controls.

Rapidly losing altitude and with one engine defunct and the other misfiring loudly, the plane skimmed the rooftops and finished up against the side of Victoria Road, killing residents Frederick and Dorothy Gill.

Once the sound of screaming, tortured metal had subdued, a strange stillness seemed to hang over the smouldering wreckage as black smoke and brick dust rose in lazy unison.

Some folk thought there was an interval of only seconds while others swear it was some minutes before, suddenly, the whole area was devastated by an ear-bursting, earth-shaking explosion. Two new parachute mines ignited amidst the blazing inferno.

Machine-gun cartridges exploded with great gusto, reminding those who witnessed the awesome spectacle " of a giant carnival firework display."

People who had been running towards the scene of the crash — which killed the four German airmen — were picked up bodily and thrown around the streets like leaves in an autumn storm. Others, standing close to windows peering out into the darkness, had faces and bodies slashed to shreds by glass.

STRICKEN

Although fire, ambulance, ARP and police organisations had been practising continuously for such an event since 1938, the forces attending the stricken surprised even the authorities.

Many of the 160 injured need never have suffered if only they had heeded the warning of the authorities. It was discovered that many of the injuries had been sustained by flying glass caused by people standing at closed windows and doorways and even running to view the crash.

Roads and normally sedate avenues around the devastated block were littered with debris. Tall trees, split and scorched by the full force of the terrible explosion, swayed drunkenly in the light early morning breeze.

Those who were in the vicinity at the time of the crash did what they could to help the wounded and bewildered homeless.

During the long night and much of the following morning the scene was one of great activity as firemen, rescue teams and police beavered away to assist the homeless into rest centres hastily commandeered around the town centre.

Amidst all this activity, the most amazing thing of all was that the second mine had failed to explode and still sat in the garden surrounded by debris.

A good many visitors actually used the thing as a makeshift seat during the night and even Det Sgt Barkway recalls resting his foot on it on several occasions thinking it was nothing more than a hot water tank from a demolished house.

Sadly the grave of Mr and Mrs Gill — England's first air raid victims — is totally unmarked with not even a small headstone to mark the spot. Their only lasting memorial is a sturdy seat almost opposite the site of their old house which bears details of the crash which really marked the beginning of the war in England.

War begins to bite

Seven months after war broke out a German mine-laying aircraft, which was apparently damaged, came down in Clacton-on-Sea. It crashed into a home and the occupants, a husband and wife, were killed as were the four German airmen.

Our local paper, the Frinton and Walton Gazette, commemorating this event in 1999 gave an account of that fateful night.

> "Shortly before midnight on Tuesday, April 30th 1940 . . . . Frederick Gill and his wife Dorothy became the first of the 60,000 civilian victims killed in the Second World War in England. They died in their Clacton home . . . . after a stricken German bomber crashed into it. First to be buried were the four German crew members carried in Swastika draped coffins".

I share this with you as my first memory of the war.

At Great Holland School we, together with the pupils from Clacton Schools, were encouraged to pick wild flowers, or buy flowers to take to the graves (which were all in one plot) of the German airmen. The idea was to encourage us not to feel bitter about these men as our enemies.

When I retired in 1990 and came to live in Kirby Cross (which is next to Great Holland) I had occasion to visit Burrsville Cemetery in Clacton. Because I am an ordained Anglican Priest I went to conduct a funeral of one of our parishioners who had once lived in Clacton. While there, I made enquiries about the grave of the airmen, and I was shown the plot. The men's bodies, of course, had been claimed by their families after the war and reinterred in their own homeland. The event of the German air crash was the precursor to the next stage of my life.

Move to a new home

After the above event it was suggested that the children in the whole area should be evacuated. The East Coast was obviously very vulnerable. My father decided we should not be split up so after a short while we moved to Laleham near Ashford in Middlesex. Here we remained for most of the war years. Although we did not suffer as much as many people we did rather go "from the frying pan into the fire". We rented a house in Laleham Road, Ashford, which was then a road leading into Laleham, a beauty spot on the River Thames.

Mary my half sister
Father's first child

My father with Mary
and Eric her husband

Opposite our house was a small forest in which was an army camp, with an anti-aircraft battery. They had quite a few Italian prisoners of war at the camp. Some of them were allowed to come to our homes for a meal now and again; they were always accompanied by an army officer. We found them to be polite and charming. The anti-aircraft battery caused us civilians a few problems with shrapnel falling on the houses. Once they fired at a V1 bomb plane and exploded it thinking it was going to fall on our homes. Sadly several of the men were killed trying to save us.

My brother Austin and myself spent quite a bit of time going down the road after an air raid and collecting all the shrapnel; we also, as part of our war effort, went from door to door collecting newspapers, an early example of recycling!! There were several aerodromes fairly near to us so we saw many Hurricanes and Spitfires go off to battle in the skies; sometimes we saw them overhead in pursuit of enemy aircraft.

When the Falklands War took place Brian Hanrahan in a news report spoke of how he watched the planes go off to the Falklands on bombing missions. He said in one report, "I counted them out and I counted them in". This brought a memory back to me of seeing many bomber planes go across the skies quite near to where we lived. As we stood in our gardens we counted the planes as they went over, and we counted them as they returned; we noted how many were missing.

Today, just one, the next day maybe five or six. How many families had lost loved ones this time?

Like many people at that time we had no air raid shelter. My parents decided we would go to bed to get as much rest as possible. If the air raids were severe, then we would come downstairs and sit together in the space under the stairs. In our house it was like a large cupboard. This part of the house was thought to be the safest place if houses nearby were bombed, or if our own dwelling received severe damage.

At some point during the war we were dive-bombed. I remember it was daytime, and we were all huddled behind the sofa which had to be pushed as close as possible to the wall. We were not hit, but it was a terrifying experience. I certainly know how people feel today who live in places of conflict. Eventually we were supplied with a Morrison table shelter, the top of which was a very thick piece of steel; if one leaned on it, it would bounce. The table was surrounded by heavy steel cage-like panels. It was meant to withstand a great deal if the house collapsed. We spent many nights in that shelter—mum, dad, my brother Austin and myself. We dozed more than slept but felt safe after a fashion.

Then Hitler sent his V1s over. These were pilotless planes nicknamed "Doodlebugs". It was only a few days since they had begun so nobody knew exactly what they were. I had gone upstairs to bed. I approached the window to pull the blackout blinds across when I saw a glow in the sky. I saw this odd looking plane going across the sky, quite low and probably only a couple of miles away. All of a sudden the engine cut-off and this plane nose dived to the ground ending in a loud explosion. At this point I became hysterical and ran to my parent's room screaming. My father slapped me across the face (the most sensible thing to do) and swore at me, "shut up, pull yourself together, some other poor b***** has been hit or killed, not you".

There was one occasion when we all had a great laugh at my expense. It was not all that long into the V1s episode. I was out in the wheat fields which were then at the back of our property. I was looking for wild flowers for a school project. The air raid warning sounded. I lay down among the wheat thinking I would not be seen by enemy aircraft. When the all clear sounded I went home. My Mother was naturally anxious about me. I told her where I had been and added, "It's alright Mum I lay down so they could not see me". Seen by whom? The planes had no pilots!!

War Time Animals

The house we lived in had a long garden at the end of which we had twelve Khaki Campbell ducks who provided us with very good eggs. My mother thought they made better cakes than chicken eggs. Today, I still enjoy duck eggs as a treat. These ducks had great characters and we gave each of them a name. If we did not feed them on time they would waddle to the back door and make their presence known. It was my job to see that they were fed. I had to boil up all the vegetable peelings and mash them up and then mix them together with bran making a palatable and nourishing feed.

We had a lovely yellow Labrador bitch called Prue, she had come with us from Great Holland. I had a cat which I had been given by the Captain at the army camp opposite our home I have already mentioned. He was transferred to another camp, and could not take the cat with him. This cat was very large and marked like a panda; he was of course named Panda when he came to me.

Prue and Panda got on so well together. One day we became aware they were making weird noises. Prue gave a sort of moaning sound and Panda yowled. About ten minutes later the air raid warning sounded. After this happened several times we became aware that in some strange way they knew that an air raid was on the way. When we eventually had our table shelter, both dog and cat would go into the cupboard under the stairs and stay there until the raid was over. Clever animals!!

At one time my brother and I had a white rabbit each. I got a cat collar for my rabbit and attached a piece of strong string to her collar, threading the washing line through a large curtain ring. I then attached the string to the curtain ring and the other end to the collar, enabling my rabbit to run up and down the garden to get exercise.

My brother Austin had four pigeons for a while; I think he just got tired of them and gave them away.

I once went fishing with a piece of thin string and a bent pin. There was a small canal nearby. I should not have been there, but I did catch a small fish, took it home, cooked it and gave it to Panda.

Wartime Schooling

I went to Sheen College in Ashford. I really enjoyed school. For one thing it gave a bit of respite from my mother's drunken ravings. I was entering my teen years which are not easy for any youngster.

My mother in those days would come home very drunk, row with my father, and scream at us children. On several occasions she would pick up a knife and threaten to kill herself, not realising she was just being what today we would call a "Drama Queen". I would become extremely upset believing she would do as she threatened.

1942 Ashford Road, Laleham
Austin (14 yrs), Mum and Helen (12 yrs)

There was only one teacher at Sheen College who seemed to take a dislike to me. Her problem with me was because I appeared to her to have no real character. I was too good, I was too quiet. If she ever knew about my home life she would have understood why. She may have had the impression that I was good but in all honesty, the outward mark of good behaviour was only to win approval. I was really quite devious.

Although home life was not happy much of the time, and in spite of my mother's problem, both mum and dad were extremely strict. For instance, we were never allowed to say "what" instead of "Pardon me" if we had not heard clearly. I remember one occasion I did say "What" and mum promptly got hold of me and threw me out the back door. Just think! That would be called abuse these days. Yet then it was accepted as the norm.

During these war years there were happy times, at least in the eyes of a child growing up. But more of this later.

CHAPTER 3

Discipline and Daily Life

Maybe it was because my parents did not want me to go astray as they had done that they were ultra strict with me; they were strict with both of us, that is Austin and myself. However, he often got away with things I could not.

Mother in particular was very controlling. I was never allowed out to play with school friends, or when I was older, to go to a youth club. For a few months I was allowed to join the Girl Guides, then no more.

It was my duty to come home from school, clean the top floor of the house and often the ground floor as well. I would then do my homework before having my tea. Maybe I would be allowed to stay up and listen to the radio before going off to bed. Once I rebelled at this treatment and threatened to leave home, whereupon my Mother told me to "go then". I did, as far as the garden gate! Realising I had nowhere to go I returned to the front door, but my mother would not let me in and I was shut in the garage for some hours. Eventually when my father came in I was let into the house but not allowed any food until the next day.

Why this kind of treatment you ask? Many children were treated like this in those days and it was not questioned. However, many years later I discovered the reason I was not allowed to mix with people or my peers outside was because of the fear, especially in my mother, that I would talk to other people about what went on at home. When I think about it I probably would have done.

In many ways I have not felt bitter or angry about those early years. I realised it taught me a self reliance, a self discipline that maybe I would not have had otherwise.

I love cooking and I am sure it is because my mother would make me prepare many of the meals at home. She would put out all the ingredients and say, "now get on with It". Being war time I learned to make a little go a long way. Years later when we were living in South Africa and during the time my father was very ill, I was glad to be able to do the cooking. Food stuffs were so much more plentiful and preparing meals was a joy to me.

As a child I was a bit of a tomboy. I loved to climb trees and make dens. When on my own I wandered in the woods or fields; I am sure this is where I developed my love of nature. I really love the creation; It speaks to me of the majesty and the glory of God even though I could not have expressed it in those terms in those days.

How I got into trouble for not behaving as a young lady should! Because my father was Jewish, women were respected and revered; he often would tell me off for not behaving as a young lady should. When I entered my teens my hair grew very long, he would not let me have it cut; "A woman's hair is her crowning glory" he would tell me. As I got older he did treat me in a respectful way. He would help me get on and off a bus. Apart from the time he slapped me on the face he never hit me. The only time I ever witnessed him hit my brother Austin was when Austin, in the middle of an argument with me, hit me hard. My Father took a newspaper and hit Austin over the head and said, "Don't you ever let me see you hit a woman again".

I cannot remember my parents ever expressing physical affection towards me, never a cuddle or a kiss. I came to know my father's respect for me as a person and as a woman. He once or twice took my part against my mother when she would not let me stand up for myself, "Let the girl explain herself". I was so grateful to him. Mum was always so unreasonable.

I loved to read and would visit the local library a great deal. I read many books about animals, and stories about people. I found comfort in reading stories where people after being unjustly treated were vindicated and in the end they came out on top. I think I saw myself in that position.

I have always been interested in people. I would sit on a bus and observe the people around me. I would imagine what their home life was like. Although I was shy and timid I could always easily talk to people. Maybe this is why my mother was so concerned that I would divulge our family affairs to outsiders.

An Interesting Friend

Walking to Sheen College each day I passed a mother and child. The child aged about ten years had cerebral palsy and rode very awkwardly on a large tricycle. Over a period of time we got talking. I found out that Yvonne was very unhappy at her school; because her speech was so slurred she was made fun of and, of course, she was very uncoordinated and could not stand unless supported.

I cannot remember if I suggested it to Mollie, but Yvonne came to Sheen College and I was delighted to look after her at school. Towards the end of the war we moved up north but Mollie and I kept up a friendship and even when we as a family went to South Africa we kept up a correspondence.

When I returned to England in 1962 one of the first things I did was to get a Green Line bus to Ashford and look up my friend Mollie. By this time she and her husband had had another child. They were told it was impossible to have another child with cerebral palsy. Sadly their second child Wendy was born with the same disease. She was about eleven years old when I saw her in 1962. Their first child Yvonne had died at the age of sixteen. Wendy was always a stronger child than Yvonne. She was able to walk more steadily and speak more clearly. Mollie developed cancer and it was around this time I discovered she was a Christian Scientist and refused much of the treatment. After she died I lost contact and her husband did not reply to my letters so I do not know what happened to him or Wendy.

Two misdemeanours and a fishing adventure

Each day as I came home from school I was not allowed to be by myself. I had to wait for Austin, that was until he left school and went to work—he left school at fourteen. One day with a couple of his school friends he went to the home of one of the pupils and I cannot remember exactly what they did, but somehow they got into the house to take revenge on this fellow pupil. This left me standing on the pavement outside the house as I could not go home on my own. The problem was that when this was reported to the headmistress it was supposed I was in on all of this. Austin pleaded with the headmistress that I had nothing to do with it and explained why. As far as the headmistress was concerned I was there. I don't know how the boys were punished I just remember I had to write out a hundred lines about not entering into other people's homes or something like that; it is all a bit vague now. I also entered into my own mischief until I got caught in the act and had to make an excuse to get out of it!

I and another girl from school went home on the long route. On the way we would knock on the doors and ask if someone new had moved in nearby to them using our own surnames. The fun was watching the person who had come to the door scratching their head and thinking hard. Of course they did not know of anyone!! I went on doing this until one day the person who came to the door was someone I knew and I had to make up a quick excuse for being there. Did I mention that 1 was devious?! Needless to say I learned my lesson; I never did it again.

Austin and I used to go fishing at Laleham in the River Thames. He did the fishing. One day he ordered me to go quickly and fill the bucket with water; he had just caught a large perch. I ran down the lock gate steps and not realising they were wet and slippery I fell into the water. I could not swim and went under the water (who was it said you go under six times and then drown?). I went under several times with Austin panicking, not able to help me. His shouting was heard and a soldier from a nearby camp came running with a stick which I grabbed hold of and he pulled me out. Instead of thanking him I went hysterical; I guess it was shock. He took us both home and by then I was able to express my gratitude. Needless to say I was afraid of water after that. I got over my fear some years later.

It missed me!

It was still war time. As I looked back some time later I realised on three occasions my life was saved, I believe by God's intervention. The river incident was one. Then there was the night a land mine exploded. We had a Jewish family billeted on us at the time; the daughter shared my bedroom and my bed was immediately under the loft door. We heard a thud upstairs as the house shook with the explosion. When we went upstairs there was the heavy loft door across my pillow. I had been allowed to stay downstairs until the raid was over!!

On another occasion I had just come past the passageway at the side of the house when the vibration from another explosion caused the landing window to shatter, just missing me!

I can't take this any longer!

So said my father, because by this time we were being bombed by the V2 rockets. We knew they were coming yet we could not hear them. Massive explosions took place in various parts of the country and many buildings were destroyed and lives lost. My father felt we had to get away from it all and, so we headed for Liverpool where one or two of his family lived. The bombing of Liverpool had ceased by this time.

We rented a large flat at the top of a town house; there was just three of us, Austin by this time had a good job with Lloyds of London and naturally stayed in London with a friend. Our flat was near Sefton Park so I walked our Labrador Prue to the park each day. It was in this park for the first time I came across a person who exposed himself to young girls and made improper suggestions. Needless to say, I turned tail and ran as fast as I could home. I think my parents reported the incident to the police. I cannot remember how long we lived in this flat but our next move took us across the River Mersey to Wallasey.

Then came the end of the war in Europe, May 8th 1945, with all the rejoicing and celebrations in the streets. The noise from the ships sirens was quite ear splitting.

Very slowly the population began to take up their lives again and as a family so did we, but more of that in the next chapter.

CHAPTER 4

A New Country and a New Life

1946-1950

My father was very disgruntled once the war had ended and life relatively began to get back to normal. He certainly did not like the political party now in power, and felt they would bring the country down, economically and in every way.

After a great deal of deliberation he made the decision to take the family to South Africa. He knew something of the country because as a young man he had worked in the gold mines in Johannesburg. I do not know when he returned to England, it could have been around the time of the First World War. I understand he served in the Fleet Air Arm, known as the Royal Naval Air

Service, during the war and that he had a bad time at Scapa Flow; he was based there.

It was during this time in the forces he met my mother—she was entertaining the troops as a singer and dancer. He fell in love with her; she was very lovely to look at, only five foot three in height and with long auburn hair.

I once saw a photo *of* her at this time in her life, it made it all the more sad to me that she became an alcoholic. She obviously fell in love with my Father.

She gave me the above information many years later in South Africa after one of the times I begged and pleaded with her to tell me why she needed to drink alcohol to the excess that she did, and I learned that she and my father never actually got married because he was already married. As a Jew in those days (and even now in many Jewish families) it was anathema to marry a non Jew. If someone did so they were excommunicated from the family and considered dead. How much worse it must have been to do what my Father did!

No wonder as I mentioned in an earlier chapter that I felt there was something unusual about our family, I can imagine why my mother found escape in alcohol. Guilt, fear and shame must have been with her for the rest of her life. No wonder my mother was so careful to see I did not mix with other people!

There is no doubt about it, my parents were well ahead of their times. Sadly, society accepts these situations now.

So came the time we sailed for South Africa, Mum, Dad, my brother Austin and myself. My elder brother Rex followed about two years later with his first wife.

My Father found an advertisement inviting people to South Africa to go into a manufacturing firm (at this time many people from Britain were going to other countries as immigrants). This was very helpful because my father had to state that he had employment to go to when he arrived in South Africa. We went to South Africa as settlers, my father intended us to become South African citizens, which we did in a few years time.

New Clothes

For me this was a very exciting time, all the preparations and all the wondering what it would be like in another country.

A short while before we sailed my mother took me shopping for some new clothes. I was so delighted, I could not remember having new clothes since I was a small child; I was now sixteen years old. I now became the owner of two new dresses, two pairs of shorts with matching blouses, a light jacket and new underwear. My delight caused me to talk about my new clothes a great deal until one day my mother said, "for goodness sake shut up, anyone would think you never had anything new". For me that was exactly how I felt. I kept quiet but hugged my delight to myself and enjoyed wearing the new clothes.

On the 8th November, 1946 we began our long journey. Apart from a few suitcases our luggage had gone on ahead. We went from Liverpool to London on the midnight train and the next morning on another train to Tilbury Docks, where we boarded the "S.S. Mataroa", a ship of the Shaw Savill Line. This ship seemed large to me but by comparison with the great liners it was small. It charged cheaper fares, maybe because this ship like others was still carrying troops.

One evening on board there was a dance and soldier approached me to ask me to dance. I was unbearably shy of men and I could not dance so I fled back to the cabin. Poor chap he must have wondered what he had done!!

Rough waters, pleasant islands

We reached the Bay of Biscay—the sea was very rough, the ship tossed up and down, it sounded as if the ship would crack in half. I learned that this was good, it meant the ship was coping with the storm and rough seas. Many people were seasick; much to my surprise I was not sick at all, though it was unpleasant with people around you being ill. There was not the luxury we have these days, the cabins held six to eight people though the sexes had their separate quarters. The dining room was laid out with long tables so when the ship lurched, one's plate slid way down the table together with others! We were eating one day (as a family we sat at the end of the table just under a porthole) and the ship lurched and the sea came in over all of us soaking us through!! Once it was over we saw the funny side of it all.

We docked at Las Palmas in the Canary Islands and were able to go ashore for the day; it was pleasantly warm. I found it so exciting seeing people from another land. Then we sailed again on the last long stretch to Cape Town.

Six thousand miles from England and we arrived. The ship was nudged into the berthing dock by two tugs. I leaned over the ships rails completely fascinated by all the activity below, so many people of different races all busy with their work on the dockside; different sounds, different languages, and different smells. Soon we were off the ship and waiting in a large hall for our luggage. While we waited we bought some peaches to eat, they were so juicy and warm, and so was the weather!! If was December, the height of summer!!

We Begin our New Life

We were met by Mr Benedel (he was the person whose advertisement my father had answered). He drove us to our new home which he had procured for us. It was a fair sized bungalow in a place called The Strand on Somerset Strand about fifty kilometres from Cape Town.

Here, apart from taking my part in helping to look after the home, I was a great deal more free than I had been in England. I was allowed out on my own. My brother Austin and myself soon made some friends; South Africans I discovered were far more outgoing than we are in England, so it is not difficult to get to know people. We were not far from the beach and sea and spent a great deal of time out in the open enjoying it all. I had never seen sea like this; it came into the shore in big rollers especially when the wind blew. It was because of these rollers I learned to swim. Our new found friends knew I was fearful of the water and had nearly drowned in the river back in England. They took me in hand and taught me. They took me out in the sea until we were waist high in water, "Come on, we will show you what to do". "Now then", said one of them, "turn your back to the sea and when the wave is about to break put your hands right out in front of you and let the water carry you to the beach". I took a bit of time to pluck up my courage, then did as I had been shown and sure enough the water carried me right up to the beach. The warmth of the water did a great deal to help remove my fear of the water. When I had done this several times and gained confidence I was then taken out beyond where the waves were breaking and they taught me how to do the crawl and breast stroke, encouraging me all the time. I finally found the confidence to swim on my own. They taught me one of their favourite games. You stand waist deep in the sea and just as the roller breaks you dive into it and come up the other side. I became quite good at this because by now I had lost my fear of being drowned. These were carefree days which did a great deal to release the stress that continued at home.

My Mother discovered how cheap alcohol was in our new country. She had easy access to it so was drunk more frequently than when we were in England. Cigarettes were also very cheap; in those days before decimal currency they only cost 2/6d for a box of a hundred. She smoked those in just over two days. How she lived as long as she did I will never understand. My father became very stressed at times trying to control her drinking as well as the times when she was very drunk and with great drama would pick up a knife and threaten to kill herself. In my naivety I believed she really could do this and I would become hysterical. My poor father was trying to deal with Mum and a teenage daughter getting very emotional. Quite a few times I saw my father crying, he must have loved her very much to have coped with it for so long.

One more move

The manufacturing business my father had been invited to join did not come to pass. I have no idea what went wrong. My father went solo and the whole family was involved when first he produced kaleidoscopes and later parrots which swung on a stand. They both sold well and obviously made enough money to keep us.

Also during this time I got myself a job at an ice cream parlour. I enjoyed this, learning to make all kinds of milk shakes and ice cream sundaes. I was highly amused when I had to make "Brown Cows"; this was Coca Cola or Pepsi Cola with ice cream in it and slightly whisked!! When that came to an end I got a job in a bicycle shop for about nine months. I quite enjoyed that as well; it taught me something of how to deal with the public.

The Chapel at Kearsney, Natal

My brother Rex in Van Der Stel

Physio Therapy and Prayer Healing block

1946 My father's passport photo

1950 My father had died

One day we learned we were moving. We moved to a place called Van der Stel only about one mile away from The Strand. Here we lived in a bungalow again. Van der Stel was an attractive village. The Hottentot Mountain Range was not far away and I loved to watch the colours change through the day. Here my Father opened up a sweet factory in which my mother worked and I did as well. The product was sweet cigarettes. My father employed six Cape Malay girls. They were so beautiful to look at. They had to remove their traditional headdress and replace it with a white head covering to protect them from the sugar dust.

Although I was unaware of it then I now realise those girls were Muslims, hence the headdress which covered their head. They also wore a yashmak covering their face below the eyes.

Then my father became ill; in time we learned he had contracted Tuberculosis. As he became weaker and weaker, my mother and I between us managed the factory, one would stay home to get the meals and one at the factory each day.

Then came the day my father died; it was my first experience of severe illness and death. My brother Austin was home from work, Mum had been drinking but was not drunk at this point, she went to the bedroom to help my father who was coughing badly then he haemorrhaged; my mother called me to fetch a bucket which I did. When I entered the room my father cried out, "Oh my God! My God!" and then collapsed and died. We rang the doctor who came eventually; I was sent to a house nearby to fetch a nurse. The doctor explained my father's lung had collapsed and his heart, which was weak, had caused him to have a heart attack.

By this time Rex my elder brother arrived with Sheila his wife. I think it was all too much for everyone and they all went out of the room. I don't remember now what the nurse said to me but she asked me to help her clean my father's body, dress him in clean pyjamas and help her to lay him out. I have no idea how I managed this except that I was always very practical, I had to be in our home situation. Strange to say but in the second Parish I ministered in I was asked by one of our church members (a lovely nurse) if I would help to lay her out when she died.

The factory was closed and as my father died intestate we were back in a rather poor state.

After the funeral my mother and I managed to get jobs in a large sweet factory not too far away. The machinery from father's factory was bought by this factory and my mother and myself worked it. It was 1950, I was just twenty years old, and wondering, "what happens now?".

Austin was engaged to be married and about six months after Dad died he went to live at the home of his future mother-in-law. I stayed at home with Mum until I was twenty one.

CHAPTER 5

A difficult situation

Now my Father had died and once his affairs were settled life for me became very stressful.

Mother was obviously grieving for my father; however the situation did not help her alcoholism.

We were both working in the sweet factory, but it was mostly I who went to work with innumerable excuses about my mother not being present. The real reason of course was she was in bed recovering from a heavy drinking bout. Before Austin left home, together we tried to help her; we even went looking for the Port, her favourite drink. We would find it hidden away in numerous places. One day we found a bottle in the lavatory cistern. In doing this we incurred her anger.

We were shouted at to mind our own business and not to dare tell her what to do. We soon came to realise that now our father had died the only restraint on her had gone.

After Austin left home I went to see our doctor and pleaded with him to give my mother some help. He made it clear to me there was nothing he could do without her consent. It then became evident to me that a real alcoholic does not think they need any help, and only when they reach the point of desperation can help be given to them.

There were days when she would have outbursts of temper for no reason that was obvious. After coming home and getting tea ready and calling Mum (she spent many hours locked in her bedroom either sleeping or drinking) she would come to the table and would suddenly throw a plate across the table straight at me. I got used to ducking and avoiding being hit. Sometimes her aim was good and I would not duck quick enough.

Then came the pleading sessions with her. Feeling so helpless and thinking something must be done I pleaded, "Mum, please why do you drink like this." "Shut up" she would reply, "you know nothing, you don't understand". She was right there. No, I did not understand. At other times it would be, "Don't you dare tell me what to do, who do you think you are? Mind your own business!"

There was one occasion when I completely lost patience and screamed at her. "Look at yourself, go on look at yourself in the mirror, you are completely evil". That really was too much and she lashed out at me. The next day she was very nice to me, gave me some money and told me to go to the pictures (Bioscope in South Africa). She was like that, when sober she was charming, generous, even kind. Drunk she was so awful.

During this time I began to think of leaving home. It was not the done thing for a woman to leave home until she was 21; my mother constantly reminded me of this.

What could I do? What about my love of animals? Perhaps I could be a kennel maid. Without telling Mum I went out and applied, I was turned down. My love of children, what about training as a nanny? Again it was no good, because having left school at 13+ and having no school certificates I was not suitable. Now what about training as a nurse? This time when I made enquiries, because my Father had T.B. there was the possibility of me succumbing to the disease (this turned out to be prophetic) and the fact of my lack of school certificates, so again if was not possible.

By now my Mother discovered what I was doing and was very angry because I had not consulted her.

Thus life went on until I reached 21. In one of her better moods my Mother asked what I would like for a present. In reply I told her I would very much like a signet ring. She promised to buy me one. When the time came she threw some money across the table and told me to get it myself. I still wear the ring today, yet the ruby set in it is the only original part of the ring. Two accidents to my hands (one in the sweet factory and one when I had to haul my dog away from a lorry) damaged the original gold ring. A new ring was bought and the ruby set into it.

In desperation I began to scan the papers for possible jobs. A large firm of Jewellers in Cape Town called Harris & Co were advertising for a trainee ledger clerk. I went for an interview and to my amazement I got the job.

Now, where to live? By this time Austin was married, his mother-in-law offered me a room in her home and I lived there for a while. 'Observatory', the name of the place where I was living, was only a short journey by train into the city.

Thus began a new type of life for me. The freedom to please myself, to mix with people, to have friends.

The owners of the Jewellery firm were Jewish men, Mr Ross and Mr Stakol. Both of them very strict with their employees, also very kind and caring. At one time while at Harris & Co I had to undergo emergency surgery. My bosses sent me to a hotel in a beauty spot called Gordon's Bay. I stayed there a week to recuperate. They paid the hotel bill and gave me extra money for anything I might need.

Who is this Jesus?

Austin's mother-in-law suggested I should attend church. At that time I understood very little Afrikaans which was the language spoken in the Dutch Reformed Church. I made the decision to go to the local Anglican Church. Now and again I went to Evening Prayer. Because church had never been part of my life it was all rather strange. I liked the hymns, it was good to sing. The service itself however did not make a lot of sense to me.

At work I was being trained by a young woman about seven years older than me, Winnie Karsten, she was a member of the Assemblies of God Church. Feb 9, 2008 I was phoned by Winnie's son. She died two years ago. I did see her five years ago when I went to South Africa.

Several anonymous phone calls were coming through for me on switchboard. As I managed this as well as my other work, I received the calls.

The caller would say what a terrible person I was for leaving my mother (by this time she had got herself a job and somewhere to live). "You are very wicked", said the caller, "How could you do such a thing?" Needless to say the person or persons who phoned were put up to it by my mother. I became very upset.

After many of these calls Winnie took the phone from me and listened to the tirade. She knew I was not making it up. It now called for an explanation of my mother's drinking problem.

Then after a particularly upsetting phone call Winnie took me aside. It was one lunch break (she could not have taken up working time to help me with my personal problems). She kept a Bible in her desk drawer, she read to me Psalm 27 (this is now one of my favourite Psalms). When she came to verse 10 she read, "when my father and mother forsake me, then the Lord will take me up" (Authorised Version). She prayed for me and my mother. She told me what I most needed in my life was the Lord Jesus. But who is this Jesus I thought, I have not heard of Him before.

Winnie suggested I apply to live at the Y.W.C.A. (Young Women's Christian Association) which was then only a short walk away from Harris & Co.

Very soon I was in the atmosphere of a Christian home. The women who ran the Y.W.C.A. were so loving and caring I was a little overwhelmed. They had Christian services once a week to which I went, thinking this was expected because I lived there. Again there was a great deal of talk about Jesus.

Ten days after I had been living at the Y.W.C.A., I discovered I had T.B. in both lungs. This became evident after a yearly check up on all employees in the city. T.B. was very prevalent in South Africa. After X-Rays which were taken in a Mobile X-Ray unit, we found out if/whether we were clear or had contracted T.B. As I was told the devastating news my whole world collapsed around me just as I had thought my life was improving. I had been suffering from throat infections quite frequently for a couple of years.

Was I going to die as my father had done? I thought. Very little time was given to sort out one's affairs. Today you are told you have T.B. and it is serious. The next day you are admitted to hospital. I spent one year in hospital.

Peggie Barrie [as she was then) the Warden of the Y.W. took me aside when I had told her I had to leave and go into hospital. We went into her private sitting room, she took her Bible and read to me of all things the 27th Psalm!! "The Lord is my light and my salvation; whom shall I fear? The Lord is the stronghold of my life; of whom shall I be afraid" . . . . "When my father and mother forsake me, then the Lord will take me up". I just sobbed; Peggie let me cry then told me how much God loved me. In what had happened, He had a plan for me.

The next day she took me to hospital, she gave me a Bible and told me to read the Gospels. She gave me a great hug and promised a place would be kept for me at the Y.W.

She and the other staff would pray for me each day. Peggie, the other staff at the Y.W. and of course my friend and colleague at Harris & Co came to see me often.

Mr Ross and Mr Stakol promised that my job would be kept open for me. I was deeply impressed that anyone should think I was worthy of such treatment.

CHAPTER 6

Hospital Life

One year under medical care and two hospitals: the first three months were spent in a hospital not far out of Cape Town. The following nine months were spent in a large government hospital near Kalk Bay and Fish Hoek, small seaside towns. The hospital itself was situated on the foothills of the mountains; it was a lovely area.

For the first five months of my time in hospital I was a strict bed patient, not allowed out of bed even to use the bathroom and the toilet. We patients only had bed baths. The one thing we could do was to wash our face and hands while sitting up in bed. Oh, the pure joy when one was eventually allowed to have a shower and to have one's hair washed after all those months.

We only had two things to keep ourselves occupied (in those months), knitting and reading. We could listen to the radio, and as long as we had it on softly during the afternoon rest hour we could keep it on. My roommate and myself followed the daily serial just as we might watch a soap on the television today. We got very involved in the story.

The government hospital was excellent in every way. The buildings were similar to an army barracks, long buildings with each building split up into two bed units and each unit painted in a pleasant pastel shade of emulsion. Each building had a veranda running along the whole length of it; it was very therapeutic. When we were eventually allowed out of bed, we thoroughly enjoyed sitting on the verandas enjoying the sun and the fresh air.

Before decimal currency came in South Africa (and it did so before Britain), we patients were able to earn ourselves some money. We were paid for knitting garments, both the men and women, if we wished to do so. We were paid one shilling and sixpence per ounce of wool we used. In my time in hospital I knitted eleven men's cable cricket pullovers. What we earned gave us enough money to buy toiletries and a few luxuries like sweets.

The treatment for T.B. was Streptomycin. This was administered by injection intramuscularly. There were a few side effects, usually headaches and muscle aches. My muscles became so hard the nurse on two occasions bent a needle on me. She swore as she had to go through the whole procedure again. It was painful but then we saw the funny side of it and had a good laugh.

I had two hundred and fifty injections of Streptomycin, then the continuing treatment was in tablet form: Pas and Izoniazide, 30 tablets of Pas and 6 Izoniazide tablets each day. This continued for two years after I left hospital.

There were two dangers with Streptomycin, you could become deaf or your eyesight could be affected. My eyes became affected so I had to come off the drug. I had to wear glasses for a while. Fortunately my eyes were not too badly affected and I only wore glasses again when I reached middle age.

When my roommate and I got to the stage of having the tablet treatment we had a competition as to who could swallow the most at one go. The Pas tablets were just a little bigger than an aspirin, the Izoniazide much smaller.

As the months went on we were given physiotherapy to build up our stamina and our muscles after being in bed for so long. In between all the medical treatment we were given occupational therapy. This was rather fun; old X-rays were cut up and turned into trinket boxes. Punching holes on the edges of the shapes we had cut out we then put the pieces together with coloured raffia. In between the pieces of X-ray plate we put pictures of flowers we had cut out of old greeting cards. These boxes when completed were very pretty. Some of the men made the most beautiful pictures with pieces of velvet and yarn or fine wool threaded through the material with a special needle. Some were pictures of a swan on a lake, others brightly coloured peacocks. These, when completed, were made into cushions or framed as wall pictures and fire screens. For some months a professional artist came in to encourage us to paint. I had a go at this but was not very good. As I look back maybe it encouraged me to (eventually) take up the idea of learning to paint once I had retired.

God speaks into my life

Many things in hospital were pleasant and kept us cheerful. Some days I experienced depression. What did the future hold? Was there any future (I was really ill)? Would I die as my father had done? The thought of dying did not worry me; it would be a way of escape from all the unhappiness in my life. The process of dying, that was another matter, especially as I had witnessed my father's death.

By now I had been told I had contracted T.B. because my father had it. Also I was in such a low state because of my situation with my mother that the disease took hold. In all the time I was in hospital my mother never came to see me. Maybe it was just as well; how would I have coped? It would have been so embarrassing if she had come and caused a scene.

In times of quiet in the hospital I carried on reading the Gospels in the Bible I had been given. I especially enjoyed the stories of people in them. When Peggie (from the Y.W.C.A.) came to see me she talked to me about Jesus, explaining that He was God's Son, that He loved me and that He died for me; that if I committed my life to Him I would become a Christian. While she or others spoke to me like this I thought I was beginning to understand, yet once they left and I tried to think about it I could not understand at all; somehow it all seemed a bit weird.

Then came the day when the depression really set in. I could not help thinking of my father, how he had died, and that made it worse. I felt very alone, helpless and hopeless and began thinking really I would like to die. After all, if I did die, all my difficulties and problems would be over. I then became very emotional and cried a great deal. Someone called a nurse, she gave me a sedative to calm me down.

That evening before we settled down for the night I began to read the Bible; it was a passage about Jesus healing someone. I cannot remember which incident it was, but in the stillness a voice that was only audible to me told me I was going to be well and that there was a purpose for me in life. This was the Lord speaking to me and somehow I realised this. At this point I had never prayed; I did not know what prayer was. As I lay in my bed and when the lights went out and the hospital and the room I was in was very quiet, I said in my heart, "I don't know who you are, I don't understand, life has no meaning for me anymore, so please take me as I am and do what you like with me". Those may not be the exact words I used but it was the gist of it, and I went peacefully to sleep.

The next day, probably because of what I had been told, I expected to feel on cloud nine. I didn't. All I knew was I had made a commitment to Christ. I had done as my friends had explained to me. It needs to be said that many people when they make a commitment to Christ do so with a realisation of their sinfulness before God. This was not so with me. I came to Christ out of a deep sense of desperation. It was many months later that the realisation of my sinfulness became apparent to me and only then did I tell God I knew I was a sinner in His sight and I thanked Him for the salvation I now had through the death of Christ on the Cross, and then made a knowledgeable commitment of my life to Christ. From then on I knew a deep peace within which filled me with wonder. That quiet peace within was something unknown to me before.

John White in his book, "When the Spirit comes with power", gives a clear picture of God's dealing with us as individuals. We are all different (unique). He writes, "If there is a guiding principle in understanding what happens when God touches someone, it

1954 Me and room mate
TB Hospital

Peggie and husband Edward
YWCA Warden

seems to be that God treats people as individuals, each having a unique history, unique problems, and a unique calling from his or her creator."

Yes, God had indeed touched my life. It was the answer to the many prayers which were prayed for me by Christians who love God and loved other people and wanted them to come to know Him for themselves. I thank God for those who prayed for me and had such an influence on my life. Do you my reader?

Quite a few Christians go through life without a real assurance of their salvation. Assurance came to me some months after I returned from hospital and got to know other Christians. One day I expressed my lack of assurance. "How can I know I am now a Christian: I don't feel any difference, how can I be sure?" The Christian to whom I was speaking took me to the Scriptures. The first letter of John, Chapter 5: and verse 10, "He who believes in the Son of God has the testimony in himself. He who does not believe God has made Him a liar, because he has not believed in the testimony that God has born to His Son. And this is the testimony, that God gave us eternal life, and this life is in His Son. He who has the Son has life; he who has not the Son of God has not life." Now I understood it is a matter of faith, I learned we have to take God at His Word. It is not how we feel, it is believing what the Bible says.

Little did I realise the importance of my life now I had become a Christian, or how my life would change in the years ahead. There was so much to learn about God and His plan and purpose for me.

The day came when I was discharged from hospital. As promised I returned to the Y.W.C.A. It took a month to get back to some sort of normality. It is not possible to spend so much time in hospital as we T.B. patients did without becoming institutionalised. To cross a busy city street was very frightening. To socialise with people each day was a strain. It does get better as time goes on. After the first month I was allowed back to work, but only for the morning, then home to rest in bed. The following month I went to work all day then home to rest in bed. This regime went on for six months then life took on a more normal pattern. It was not an easy lesson but I learned to be patient.

The weekly services at the Y.W. became a blessing to me. I began to understand a lot more about how to live as a Christian. Some lessons were hard to learn, for instance how to be obedient to Christ's commands. Like most people I failed many times. I began to learn how to come to Christ and confess how I had failed, how I had sinned, how He accepts us, understands, forgives and restores us again.

Becoming a member of a Church

It soon dawned on me I had never been baptised. Through reading the Bible and through teaching I came to understand it is a scriptural command. Cape Town Cathedral, St Georges, was the place at which I chose to worship. A godly and prayerful man, Tom Savage, was the Dean of the Cathedral at the time. I went to see him and discuss with him what I should do. He explained I should receive instruction and I joined with others in an instruction class. Looking back those times were very precious. The teaching I was given was so valuable. On the 21st August 1955 in the presence of a packed congregation I stood at the large Baptismal Font and proclaimed my faith in Christ as my Lord and Saviour. I had been forewarned it was to be a broadcast service and I knew many people were listening. Was I nervous? Yes, I certainly was nervous, my legs shook, yet the joy of what was taking place overcame the nerves. In the afternoon of that same day with others I was confirmed and became a member of the Anglican Church. It was a good service yet nothing could compare with what had taken place in the morning. I learned so much about prayer and living the Christian life from Tom Savage for which I have always been grateful.

There was one sad note to that lovely day. My mother promised me she would come to see me baptised. She was most unhappy that I had become a Christian and went for me many times. It was all nonsense, she thought. She did not turn up for the service and later I was told she was picked up early in the day in one of the city streets blind drunk. I do need to tell you that some years later when I had returned to England she wrote to me. In the letter she wrote, "I will never understand why you did what you did, but I do wish your brothers had the peace you have." I held on to those words realising that even if she did not understand she had seen something of what Christ could do in a person's life. As far as I knew she did not come to know Christ for herself. I had conversations with her in which I explained what happened to me and what I knew God had done in my life. She died at the age of 77 in a nursing home. The last time I saw her was the day I sailed to England in 1962. After my Baptism and Confirmation I began my Christian pilgrimage and had taken the first steps in God's call in my life.

CHAPTER 7

Life with a purpose

Life was becoming so different now. Work as a Ledger Clerk was fulfilling and Instructive.

Harris and Co (Jewellers) did hold my job for me, as they had promised. Winnie Karsten who taught me my work was now able to go home to have her family. Someone else was employed in my place as a trainee Ledger Clerk and I took over Winnie's position, it was a responsible job which entailed interviewing new customers who wanted to open accounts (items they wished to purchase often cost hundreds of pounds), keeping all the customer accounts—in those days it was done on a Roneo system which was a challenge; today it would all be done on a computer! Everything was double checked, the bosses were not well pleased if an error was found. The sales books had to be kept up to date each day and letters written to customers who did not keep up payments on their accounts. Above all this my junior colleague and myself had to have a full! knowledge of the stock we held, which was very varied.

We stocked beautiful china and glass, clocks and watches apart from all the beautiful jewellery. We had a watchmaker on the staff. I learned a great deal from him about good watches. Years later, on my first trip overseas from England I bought myself a good watch in Geneva.

Some knowledge gained was through what appeared a strange request. A request came from the shop for us to check if we had any pigeon clock dials in stock. My face must have been a picture as I hastily asked, "What are pigeon clock dials?"

During the rest of my time at Harris and Co, regular checkups, X-rays and screening had to be done to see if the T.B. was in check. This continued until 1962 when I returned to England.

Plans to help my Mother

In chapter five I mentioned problems I had with my mother's alcoholism. Now settled myself and physically much stronger I made contact with Mum and tried to do something to help her. She had a couple of periods of employment but lost the jobs because of being drunk at work. There was an advertisement in a Cape Town paper asking for an assistant housemother at a Jewish orphanage. What a good idea I thought. Maybe because of my father being Jewish, this might please her. I discussed it with her and she agreed this would be good. I applied on her behalf and she was employed.

Sadly, twelve days later I got an anxious call from the Matron, "Would I go immediately, my mother was behaving in an erratic and strange way and the staff did not know what to do". On investigation of her room we discovered she had been drinking eau de cologne because she had no access to any other alcohol. She was only going to receive a salary at the end of the month so could not buy any. Needless to say that was the end of that—no place to live, no work.

The next efforts were to encourage her to go to A.A. (Alcoholics Anonymous). Her immediate reaction was to insist she did not need help, and to "leave her alone".

Determined to do something I approached the Cape Town branch of A.A. They were very kind and helped me to understand that alcoholism is a disease. My mother had to come to the point where she had come to an end of herself and knew she could not go on without help. That was so helpful in understanding my mother. Together we devised a scheme whereby a member of the A.A. would go with me under the guise of being a boyfriend. I would introduce him to my mother and hopefully in time she could get to trust him and he would be able to help her. Sadly, this did not work out, the "boyfriend" went back to drink himself.

It was at this point I came to realise that there was nothing else I could do to help my mother with her alcoholism. It was at this time whatever frustration, anger and bitterness I felt for her left me and was replaced by a love for her that was expressed in my prayers for her to become a Christian, to know His love for her, and to have his peace in her heart. I visited her when I could; I spoke to her about how Christ had changed my life. At times she would reply, "What need did you ever have of forgiveness?" "I will never understand what you did"; she meant she could not understand why I had become a Christian.

In time she became eligible for the South African pension. By now my eldest brother had remarried after being divorced, he and his second wife had bought a home with a granny flat attached. They opened up their home to her. It was here she lived until, in her seventies, she became too poorly and spent the rest of her days in a nursing home until she died in 1972. She was 77 years old.

At this time I had returned to the U.K. to train for full time ministry. My last visit to my mother was in 1962 on my way back to the U.K. The ship docked at Cape Town for a few days, so I took the opportunity to go and see her and say "Goodbye". I did not get to her funeral. I was in my first parish in Plymouth. A telegram arrived to inform me my mother was very ill in hospital. Two church members very kindly bought me a short stay plane ticket to fly out to South Africa to see Mum. A further telegram came two days later to inform me she had died. It was considered impracticable for me to travel all that way. The flight was cancelled. I was relieved my mother was no longer suffering. My great sadness was I did not know if she had ever come to know Jesus as her Saviour. I always had a vision of being at her side when her earthly life was over and helping her to commit her life to Christ. Friends helped me to see I had to leave that in God's hands; only He knows ultimately.

Outdoor life

Cape Town has a Mediterranean climate, thus a lot of time is spent outdoors. Work ceased at lunchtime on Saturdays, my friends and I met together for swimming parties to one or other of the lovely beaches all around the coast of False Bay. Some evenings we had great fun going to a beach nearby. We would have a time of Bible Study, prayer and singing and then enter into a watermelon feast and beach games. One of our great games was to see who could walk the furthest along the beach on their hands. It takes a lot of balance. I got quite good at this, but I never won!! Once a month on my afternoon off from work I would take a bus to a place called Camps Bay. Camps Bay had very large boulders, the sea would crash over them and cause the spray to rise high in the air. The power of the sea spoke to me of God's power, as did the mountains along this part of the coast.

After church on Sundays friends got together and would take a bus to the lower slopes of Table Mountain and walk along through the pine trees. The aroma of the pines was lovely. At other times we would walk up Signal Hill near to Lions Head at the side of Table Mountain.

in 1955 several of us younger people from Cape Town Cathedral went to an Easter Camp. On Easter morning we got up at 5 am, gathered together in the cool of the early morning and just as the sun rose and tipped over the mountains we all stood and sang, "Jesus Christ is risen today"; this was a very moving experience. In 1957 with a few friends I went to a Holiday Camp in Ceres, a lovely part of the Cape, ringed by mountains 2000m high. Here we revelled in swimming in the river, climbing in the mountains (but not too high!), and generally enjoying ourselves. They were great days.

Life as a Christian

Each day as I stepped into my spiritual pilgrimage it became evident there was so much to learn, in fact we never stop learning, our God has so much to teach us. We do not become a Christian and that is that. We are saved to serve, to serve our Lord God and our fellow men and women. I gradually learned how God teaches us and feeds us each day as we read His Word and spend time in prayer.

Living as a Christian brings its own challenge, as does trusting God in all situations. We also find that some lessons have to be learnt again and again. We come to realise how patient God is with us, because He loves us so much. He does not give up on us however many times we fail Him. It was my experience and it still is that God speaks to us in every experience through His Word, and sometimes through other people.

One day during my time at Harris & Co I was asked by Mr Ross to give a message to one of the shop assistants: she happened to be in the stock room at that moment. He wanted to see her before she returned to the shop. I passed on the message which irritated her and she refused to go. When she did not turn up as requested Mr Ross asked me if I had passed on the message. Miss Talyard did not ask what he wanted to see her about. This caused quite a situation. Mr Ross asked me several times if f had done as he asked. I told him I had done so. I did not want to tell him she was reluctant to go because she was busy at the time. This went on for a couple of days; Mr Ross became rather cross and obviously did not believe me. Because I became upset Winnie Karsten went into Mr Ross and explained what had happened. She realised he was getting to the place where he might well have fired me, thinking I had lied to him. Once he knew what had happened he went to speak to Miss Talyard who then became furious with me, thinking I was the one who had told him. The situation did eventually resolve itself. I realised for the first time how I was affected by my past as a child, of being in trouble and being punished for something I had not done at all. If I am in the wrong I can take the consequences but being accused for something I had not done really gets to me.

The evening of the day this situation blew up while I was at a Bible Study. The passage we were reading came from Peters 1st Letter, Chapter 2, and these words spoke to me, "what credit is it, if when you do wrong and are beaten for it you take if patiently? But if when you do right and suffer for it you take it patiently, you have God's approval." Down through the years on the odd occasion I have been accused of something I have had nothing to do with at all, I have been really hurt and then the words of Peter have come back to me. How gracious is our God!

CHAPTER 8

The Healing Home

"One more step along the World I go
And it's from the old I travel to the new,
Keep me travelling along with you."

These words come from a children's hymn. They express what was about to take place next in my pilgrimage.

Settled and happy, so why this inner awareness that there was something else for me to do? It expressed itself in a desire to give back to God what He had given to me. Salvation, peace of mind and heart, and a purpose in life; plus a great measure of health. Of course we cannot give back to God what He has given to us; we can in gratitude give ourselves to God for His service.

Because this awareness did not go away, I began to pray about it, yet the more I prayed the more my thoughts become muddled and confused. Realising I needed some guidance I went to see Tom Savage—he was the Dean of Cape Town Cathedral—a very wise and prayerful man. He discerned God was calling me to do something specific. He advised me to remain prayerful and ask God to show me what it was He wanted me to do. He prayed with me and sent me away with some literature on seeking God's guidance.

For some time I continued to pray, until one day I picked up a magazine in the Cathedral about a Home of Divine Healing. In the magazine there was an advertisement for a vacancy for a member of staff, it is very difficult to put into words but I knew somehow this was the answer to my prayer.

Because I was so young in faith and spiritual understanding I returned to Tom Savage for help. The Healing Home—called Kearsney Home of Divine Healing—was 1,000 miles away in the Province of Natal. There were questions to be considered. What about my Mother? I was helping to support her financially; I would not be able to continue that support. To become a member of a community would cut down one's finance considerably. What about my health? At that point I was still on TB medication in tablet form. Supposing I had to have training and would be refused because of my lack of schooling?

Tom Savage in his wisdom said, "If God is calling you to take this step, you will have to trust Him to take care of all these things and He will if this is His plan for you."

The next step was to write to the Warden of Kearsney and apply for the position advertised. The staff at Kearsney were made up of people from different denominations, Anglicans, Baptists, Methodist, and one or two from Pentecostal churches, all different age groups.

The Warden Mr Winkley who was an ordained Anglican Priest was going to be in Cape Town for a Conference. He answered my letter and requested to come and see me. As we sat and talked in the lounge of the Y.W.C.A. he told me all about the Healing Home, the people there, and why they were there. Part of the home was run on the lines of a nursing home. These people were permanent. Others came for a time to seek physical and spiritual healing. Quite a few were physically and mentally disabled. Incorporated into the whole set up was a physiotherapy room and an occupational therapy room in the grounds. Then there was also a home within the extensive grounds where African children came who had T.B. in their limbs.

They were ministered to physically and spiritually but had to live in their own compound because white and black could not live together. These were still the days of apartheid.

As we talked Mr Winkley said he felt I was the right person to be there. I would begin by working in and organising the general office. I would be part of the Community, share a bungalow with a nurse on the staff and learn about the healing ministry. I expressed the same questions I had discussed with Tom Savage. Mr Winkley told me the same thing, that if this was what God intended He would take care of these concerns, but I had to trust Him to do so. He then asked me if I would like him to pray for me for complete physical healing. In answer I said, "Yes I would."

This was at the time a strange experience for me. As Mr Winkley prayed and laid hands on my head there was a strong sense of warmth going through my whole body. As I got up from where I had been kneeling I felt very light headed. This soon passed off yet the feeling of warmth remained for quite a while through the day.

Mr Winkley returned to Natal and in a short while a letter came to tell me I had been accepted for the position for which I had applied. "One more step along the World I go".

What next? I had to give in my notice to Harris and Co. To tell the Y.W. I would not be living there much longer.

Peggie, the Y.W.C.A Warden mentioned in Chapter 5, was very pleased that God was working in my life. A couple of other members of staff questioned the rightness of this. At one point they did all they could to dissuade me. Now, here was another lesson to learn. Here were people older and wiser than me; who did I listen to? Listen to God was the answer, listen, pray. Are you sure I asked myself? Yes, I was sure. So in spite of conflicting advice I went ahead, yet feeling sad I may have hurt those who thought they were giving me the right advice.

So, what about those questions I had? It was around this time my brother Rex remarried and my mother went to live in the granny flat at the side of their home. Rex said he did not expect me to continue to contribute to her upkeep.

I went for a routine check up at the hospital. It was one of the times I was screened. The consultant asked me where I had the T.B. As he was the first consultant who discovered it was in both lungs I was puzzled. When I questioned this he said he knew one lung was affected much more than the other. When I told him which one he replied, "This is strange, I cannot see the scarring that was there." It was then I knew God had settled that question!!

Then the concern about training was not a problem. It was not needed for the office work. All else was learned in my time at Kearsney.

Leaving Harris and Co was sad. Mr Ross and Mr Stakol were very kind to me as were my work colleagues: Winnie Karsten who had first talked to me about Jesus, Peggie at the Y.W. who was mainly instrumental in leading me to my commitment to Jesus as Lord and Saviour. But I did not lose touch with these lovely people. When I went on holiday I returned to Cape Town and visited the folk at the firm; they greeted me open arms. Mr Stakol, although a Jew, joked with me about my Christian work. "You won't preach at me will you?" he said. In the shop, where I bought a watch for a friend, he spoke to the shop staff to tell them how proud he was of me in what I was doing. I had told him quite clearly I had become a Christian.

I met up with Peggie and her husband (she married a Baptist Minister before I had left Cape Town) quite a few years later in Natal, when she was helpful in another step along the way.

Now here I was after a thousand mile journey in a most beautiful part of Natal. Kearsney Healing Home was set 50 miles from the city of Durban in very large grounds surrounded by sugar cane plantations. The Main House was just like a British stately home. There were lovely garden areas, and beautiful trees. Beneath my room in the shared bungalow was a pineapple patch. I call it that because although large it was not a field. If I leaned out of my window I could almost reach the pineapple plants.

So began my next step along the way. It was as would be described today as a steep learning curve. I spent eighteen months at Kearsney. The first six months in the office, which was busy for most of the day dealing with the residents' various needs. The office held the money for some residents who were mentally unstable or severely disabled. Help had to be given to them to help them manage their money. Part of my brief was to seek to get alongside the residents and the short term visitors.

The next six months I spent in what was known as the Prayer Healing Office. Here was a ministry of writing and answering letters. People wrote in asking for prayer and advice on all kinds of problems: physical, mental and spiritual. For this I was led by a lovely member of staff—he was the deputy warden—a Baptist Minister. His name was Eric Fleischman. Because he was of German origin he had been interned during the Second World War. It was he who threw me "in at the deep end." He asked me to lead the early morning prayer service where residents and people who had requested prayer in their correspondence were prayed for. I was so nervous and felt so inadequate. In answer to my expressed fear Eric said to me, "You believe God led you here, you feel you don't know what to do. Go and ask the Holy Spirit to show you how, then I will give you some constructive criticism". I did as he said. I put together and led that first service with beating heart and shaking knees, and even managed to carry on when a dear elderly blind lady—Mrs Buxton called out in a very aristocratic voice "I cannot hear you, please speak up."

Eric did give me constructive criticism and was so helpful then and subsequently when he asked me to prepare and give a talk at the evening devotional meeting. During my time at Kearsney I frequently led a service or gave a talk at one of them. In all these years I have never lost my nervousness of talking or preaching. Is this God's way of keeping His children from becoming self reliant?

My last six months were back in the office, as well as this I now helped in the Ministry of Healing at one service or another.

One day I was called to be alongside Mr Winkley as he ministered to an Anglican Priest who was dying. Sadly, I cannot remember his name. We saw him in the chapel and sitting in his wheelchair on one of the verandas a few times, during his stay at Kearsney. He had been an

Army Chaplain in the Second World War. He had been persecuted in a Japanese Prisoner of War Camp. His tongue had been cut out. His hands and wrists bore terrible scars where he had been strung up in a tree in a mock crucifixion. He was such a dear gentle man. He bore no bitterness or hatred towards those who had treated him so badly. Now here he was dying.

We had a short service in his room. I stood at his side as instructed and made the answers he would have made had he been able to speak. Mr Winkley and I prayed for him and laid hands on him. He was very peaceful and that afternoon he died. This was a very emotional experience to enter into. It was also a great privilege to minister to a man who had fought for his country and who had suffered immensely.

There was also the time I learned the power of Jesus name. I woke up one night with a dreadful and tangible sense of something evil. I could not get back to sleep as whatever it was seemed all around me. Instinctively I picked up my Bible asked God to protect me and held my Bible to myself. I don't even know what I thought would happen. The fear I felt went away, and I went back to sleep.

It seemed right to go and discuss this with someone and I went to Eric Fleischman in the morning. He knew what had happened. Up to that point I was unaware of people being possessed. He questioned me if I had been in the company of one of the residents; I had. This particular person would approach with glaring eyes and at times be quite belligerent. Sometimes would oppose what was being said in Chapel. Please understand this person was not an evil person. Because of her past and what she had been involved in she was now possessed. She often approached me with a goading and mocking attitude. Eric explained that the next time this person came to see me I was to lift her up in prayer quietly and use Jesus' name.

One day she walked across the grounds towards the office; as she approached I could see here was the time I was to put into action what Eric had instructed me. She approached with glaring eyes; I began to pray quietly for her using Jesus' name, then as she came near she visibly wilted and just quietly asked me for what she wanted. Another lesson learned!

I also learned about the ministry of deliverance from evil. It is a gift some Christians are given. Because I came to know I did not have this gift I have never tried to use it, it is an area of ministry that is not to be entered into lightly, though there have been times in my ministry I have received and have been able to use a Spirit of Discernment; a gift I asked God to give to me.

The children at Ekuphilisweni Green Pastures

Me with a few of the children

Then there was the lovely African children's part of Kearsney. All of them suffering from T.B. in their limbs. The African name for this part of the home was Ekuphilisweni (Green Pastures); it was truly a lovely place. It was also the first Missionary Home of Divine Healing in the World.

A colleague and myself went down to the children each week. We spent time with them teaching them Bible Stories, praying with them and playing with them. Some could not walk at all, some were able to walk with medical aids, others were able to walk. These were very precious times with those dear children.

To get down to Green Pastures we walked through an avenue of Guava trees, very attractive with a pleasant aroma issuing from them. These Guava trees had two crops of fruit each year. The first crop was rather wormy, the second crop were beautifully sweet with a strong flavour. We loved to gather them and enjoy them. Now in England for an occasional treat I will buy myself a tin of Guavas!!

Among those trees and other trees in the grounds lived Boom Slang—Boom = tree, slang = snake. These snakes did no harm unless they were frightened or touched. For instance, if one slipped off a branch and you were underneath and it fell on you it would bite, unless of course you managed to shake it off in time.

Some of the Africans were very clever at getting rid of these snakes for which we were grateful. Frequently they would knock the snakes out of the trees and then kill them.

Rosamund Oxlade, the nurse with whom I shared a bungalow in the grounds, was very frightened of spiders and moths. It fell to me many times to get rid of the offending creatures. Some of the spiders were poisonous (I came to know which were harmful) and I could deal with them. The moths received kinder treatment. They were rather large, a body as thick as a small finger, with a wing span of approximately five inches. Like all moths they were attracted by light and would hover around the electric lamps before settling down. Armed with a dish cloth I would cover them and put them out in the grounds. Some nights when we were getting ready to retire to bed, a scream would come from Rosamund's room, and I would go into action!!

Sometimes while walking round the sugar cane plantations we could hear rapid swishing sounds. These sounds were snakes slithering away as they heard us approaching; they were more frightened of us than we of them.

Let me tell you about the moth that disrupted an Evangelistic meeting. An American preacher had come to speak at this meeting. As he was speaking one of these large brown and black moths got into the hall. As all moths do it hovered round the light, it also took a fancy to the speaker's head! Finding himself nonplussed he said, "Say, they're cute little fellows aren't they?" A short while later the moth was circling the speaker's head all the time. He obviously could not take it any longer. "I say. What do you do, shoot 'em?" At this point someone got up and removed the offending creature. (You have to imagine the American accent as you read this).

In this rarefied atmosphere with all the fellowship of Christians from different denominations, our times of Bible Study and prayer together I learned a great deal. Not only did I learn but experienced that "We are all one in Christ Jesus." As Paul wrote to the Christians in Galatia. Galatians 3, verse 28. "There is neither Jew nor Greek, slave or free, male nor female, for you are all one in Christ Jesus". Different though we are in many ways, in Christ we were united as one. God was preparing me for the future.

One day I had a visit from three ladies from the city of Durban and this was the beginning of the next step along the way.

CHAPTER 9

The Hostel Warden

1958-1961

"Helen, there are three ladies from the Durban Y.W.C.A. to see you. I have put them in the sitting-room in the main house," said my colleague.

I made my way there from the bungalow I shared with Rosamund. I was puzzled. I did not know anyone in Durban. Was this anything to do with the Y.W.C.A. I had lived in previously in Cape Town before I had come to Kearsney?

As I entered the sitting-room I saw my visitors were very smartly dressed and looking rather official! They introduced themselves as Trustees of the Y.W.C.A. in

Durban. They has come to see me because the Y.W. Hostel in Durban was in need of a new Warden. They went on to explain that they had heard that I was a suitable person for the situation. My immediate reaction to their offer was to say, "I do not have the training for this situation". They then went on to explain I had the qualities that were required. I had the ability to manage; I was capable of giving spiritual and moral guidance, which would be required when dealing with young women. They also believed I could manage the household staff of twenty two Africans, half of whom were Zulu, and half were Xhosa.

The residents were young women between the ages of sixteen and twenty five; some of whom were students and some working women who would be far away from home.

The Apartheid system of government was in operation in those years, therefore all the residents were white. Thankfully, as I write this, residents in the Y.W.C.A. Hostels are mixed; Black: white and Cape Coloured (people of mixed race).

There were also two African women with whom I would be working. They were both trained social workers. Their work was outside the Hostel. They worked outside the city in the townships running Y.W.C.A. Youth clubs, and caring for the welfare of the young people there.

After consulting my trusted colleagues at Kearsney and much prayer it became clear this was the next step God wanted me to take. Saying goodbye to colleagues and residents was not easy. I had learned a great deal in the eighteen months spent at Kearsney, and I was grateful. Several people had become good friends and remained so for many years.

I made the journey to the lovely city of Durban on the East Coast of South Africa. The hostel was an attractive building with Dutch gables. A sloping lawn went down to a very busy road fronting a bay with a marina. Many times there were flocks of pink flamingos flying over the bay, they appeared as a large pink cloud above the sea.

My predecessor was there to welcome me and see me settled into the warden's flat which overlooked the beautiful bay. I cannot remember how long she stayed but it was long enough to show me all the things I had to cope with. At first it seemed rather daunting. There were ninety nine residents. Getting to know their names was a challenge! I had been told that to have this position I would have to learn to drive. Now that was a challenge! I had never thought of or wanted to drive. However, lessons were booked up for me. With extreme nervousness I took the course. A friend from Kearsney had a cottage at a seaside hamlet nearby, she came over and let me have plenty of practice in her car. The book keeper in the Y.W. also let me practice in her car. To my astonishment I passed the test the first time. In those days the test was very strict, especially where parking was concerned. The instructor assured me I was going to be a good driver. The encouragement I needed!

The day I passed the test my colleague Eve, the book keeper, sent me out immediately to go to the Council Offices to pay the government tax for the African staff. This meant I had to go in the hostel car down the side drive and filter into the heavy traffic travelling along the Esplanade. With a thudding heart, gritted teeth and weak knees I did it. It was only afterwards I realised that Eve had got me to do the best thing possible. It would have taken me ages to pluck up the courage on my own, if at all!

I spent three years in Durban. Years of many lessons which were preparing me for the future. Years of happy and sad memories; again this was a time of learning and preparation for the future.

What does a Hostel Warden do?

The warden had varied responsibilities. Letting the rooms, interviewing the parents, or the young women who applied to come. There had to be certain rules and regulations. It is a Christian organisation; the residents had to accept this though not all were Christian. A

Christian service was held once a week. It was hoped all would attend, but it was not insisted on. It was the Wardens responsibility to lead the service; also to arrange guest speakers each week, and to speak at the service herself when a speaker was not available.

There was the responsibility for all the household staff: the chef and all the assistant cooks etc. There was a gardener who, as well as keeping the grounds in order, also accompanied the warden each week to the Indian market to purchase all the fruit and vegetables. This involved an early morning rise at five o'clock! It was here I found Joseph (not his real name) very helpful. He was able to tell the ripeness of certain fruit and vegetables, especially squash (pumpkin) and watermelon, as well as other things. I was so amused to see him lift a watermelon for example onto his head and give it a soft bump. In this way he was able to tell whether it was suitable to buy. He was also a great help because he could speak more than one African language and could bargain with the Indian stall holders who were quite crafty and could have cheated me. I certainly valued Joseph.

Creature Hazards

It was part of the warden's work to see that the property was kept in good order, inside and outside.

There was a constant battle to keep cockroaches under control. Usually "creepy crawlies" did not bother me, but I have to admit cockroaches gave me shivers down my back. Even with all the insecticide we used—it, was full strength D.D.T. In those days, one would go into the kitchens at night to hear and see the baby cockroaches running across the floor. One day when walking down the esplanade outside the hostel I looked down to see some fully grown cockroaches making their way along the pavement! Was this a small version of one of the plagues of Egypt in the days of Pharaoh!!

There was the day when one of the residents came to inform me she had discovered a bed bug in her bed. That was major, it meant the room had to be sealed and fumigated, and left for a whole week before the room could be used again.

One evening there was an almighty scream from upstairs. I ran up the stairs to find a hysterical resident. As she was about to get into the bath she found a rather large rat swimming in it. I called one of the African staff who came and killed it.

Durban is a place of high humidity, because of this we had a constant battle with mosquitoes.

African Culture

The African staff called me Inkosasana. The word means Princess, Madam, Miss or unmarried woman. By using this name for me they were treating me with respect.

I found out one of the older African men (Samson, a Zulu) was in charge of the other men. It was a little bit like being a foreman who saw that they behaved, and was their spokesman if they had any problems or complaints, which he brought to me. I would communicate through him anything I needed them to do.

Then there was Frances. She was a Xhosa lady, and was in charge of the women. She was always such a gracious soul.

I had not been in charge for very long when two things began to concern me. Remember these were the days of Apartheid. I found that when the women saw me or had to approach me in the corridors, or they had to come to my office for something, they would curtsey. I was horrified. I did not want this deference because I was white. I approached Frances, telling her I did not regard them as black and me white. I was not superior to them. "Inkosasana, you must not stop them from doing this. It is their culture, in their Kraals (villages) they are expected to curtsey to their elders". After this

I had to accept it, but I did not like it. One day when I was speaking to one of the younger African female staff who cleaned the bedrooms, I became aware she did not answer me after giving her some instruction, she also appeared to look very sullen. I consulted Frances. "Frances, why is Sarah (not her real name) so cross looking and why does she not say anything when I speak to her? Please can you tell her if she is not happy being here she may go. I know that she can earn a bigger salary in one of the hotels doing the same thing." "Oh, Inkosasana, she is only being polite to you. At home in her family, if she is being instructed she must not answer or smile, if she does it would be rude or insolent". Another lesson learned!!

In the morning while working in my office I would hear the staff singing at their morning prayers. The Zulus in particular naturally harmonise, rather like the Welsh. To listen to them each day I found quite lovely.

Drama

When the students who were at college went home at the end of term, I had to let their rooms to keep up the revenue. Older women would come and stay for a week or so. Over the Christmas period I would arrange a Christmas lunch for local women who were on their own.

I will never forget one Christmas day. There were forty women in the dining-room enjoying their meal. I heard a loud scuffle outside in the hallway. I went to investigate and found to my horror, one African chasing another with an axe in his hand; the man he was chasing was screaming. How do I deal with this? Was my immediate thought. As the two men ran towards the front entrance I managed to ask one of the waiters to keep the door of the dining-room closed. I ran to the outside front of the building to see that the two men were now struggling on the pavement. I then ran back inside to phone the police. I was told they could not come as they were too busy. I went back to the two men who were now screaming at one another. I could not speak their language but shouted at them to stop. For some reason or other the one with the axe had not used it, but I could not be sure he would not do so. I hastened back to the phone, "If you do not come someone will be murdered and it will be your fault." This time the police did come and broke up the situation. The men were taken off to prison. In the meantime the police explained to me that both men were under the influence of Dacca (marijuana). Unfortunately, they had to be dismissed from their employment at the Y.W.

Another day of drama occurred when the boyfriend of one of the residents came to visit her. Because he was drunk she urged him to leave the premises. He became angry, threw his arm backwards into a plate glass window and cut two arteries. The girlfriend screamed. Eve (my colleague) and myself ran to see what had happened and I had to put my first aid into action. Eve quickly went to get the first aid box. With great difficulty, because the boyfriend was fighting and yelling, I managed to get a tourniquet on his arm to stop the flow of blood. It seemed there was blood everywhere. We finally got the young man to my office and made him drink some black coffee to sober him up. It had no effect whatsoever. I realised we needed to get him to hospital. Again with great difficulty we got him into the car. I drove while Eve sat with him in the back holding him down. At every traffic light he tried to get out of the car. Fortunately the city hospital was not too far away. The medics patched him up, but they had to sedate him first, he was still fighting. Once seen to we had to get him to where he lived. That was easier, by now he was decidedly calmer. We left him with a couple of friends who put him to bed. Before we got him to the hospital we had to get two friends of his girlfriend to stay with her as she was hysterical. She was naturally very worried about the damage her boyfriend had done to himself. She also felt I would possibly ask her to leave because of all the trouble caused. This did not happen.

The following day, looking a bit pale and his arm in a sling, the boyfriend arrived at the hostel with an enormous bouquet of flowers for Eve and myself. He was so sorry for the trouble he had caused. When he saw all the blood splashed up the outside wall he realised what a problem we'd had with him. He explained he had been out with a few friends for a drink and they has spiked his drink with some drug and that is why he was in the state he was. He was a very nice young man, also one of the local rugby players, physically big and strong, no wonder we had such a difficult time controlling him.

There was another day when Samson (the man who was in charge of the male staff) came to me to tell me two of the men were fighting and he was helpless to stop them. I went out to the courtyard to find two rather large Zulu men trying to throttle one another. I could not speak Zulu (I was having lessons). All I could do was shout at them very loudly, they did understand English. To my surprise they did stop but not before one turned round hovered over me and shouted in Zulu. For a moment I thought I was about to be attacked, and sent up more than one arrow prayer! The situation did calm down. I then asked Samson to take over. Later Samson told me I should dismiss the man who has started the whole thing. Another drama over!

When one needs wisdom

Two rather anxious residents came to see me. They had found out that two students who had come from

Johannesburg had each got a gun. I called the two young women to my office and explained to them we did not allow guns on the premises. They explained that where they had come from they needed the guns to protect themselves. After assuring them that was not necessary in the city of Durban, they handed the guns over to me which I locked into the safe until they eventually returned home to Johannesburg.

After one of the Monday Services two girls came to see me. The speaker that evening had warned the residents about the danger of the occult. They wanted me to know they saw nothing wrong with it. I told them from the bible that we are warned not to dabble with the occult. I explained about the dangers and reasoned with them. They were not too pleased and told me in no uncertain terms that I was old fashioned, and that they thought I was over reacting.

Some months later (they had left the hostel by then) they came to see me because they were frightened at what was happening to them. One lass explained she was frightened because wherever she went she felt an overpowering presence behind her as if someone was following her. I advised her to go and see a Christian minister who would help her. I did not know if she took my advice. Sadly I heard she had taken her own life. Sometime later I was informed that the other young woman had a mental breakdown and was in a psychiatric hospital. I was very sad but felt I had done my best by warning them of the dangers of the things they were entering into. I knew they had been going to séances and had been playing with a Ouija board.

Some of the residents, though not many, came from broken homes. My own background was useful. When they realised I had not come from a privileged background they found it easier to trust me with their problems and I was able to help them.

I found I needed wisdom in every situation; as I prayed and trusted God I found the right thing to say or the right advice to give.

Life as a warden was not all drama, or difficult situations. There were many joyful occasions: celebrating a birthday, an engagement, and now and again a wedding. Sometimes I felt like a surrogate mother.

The Y.M.C.A. was not too far away. The warden of the Y.M. and myself as warden of the Y.W. were invited to the home of a professor. He was from the Indian University in the city. We were invited to an evening meal and to meet an Indian Swami. If I remember rightly he was Hindu. Here was another occasion to find out about another culture. The professor, his wife and two daughters lived in a wonderful home. They were obviously well off; we had a sumptuous traditional Indian meal. Although I enjoyed the curry it was far too hot for me. I only managed to get through it by sipping cold water!! The main meal was followed by very sweet sweetmeats, and finally by very sweet tea.

We moved to the sitting room to listen to the Swami. He must have been speaking about his faith and his position as a Swami. All these years later I cannot remember any details of what he spoke to us about. Maybe it was above my head!!

There was one thing that came as a shock to me that evening. Not wanting to be impolite I did not express how I felt. The professor's wife and two daughters, dressed in exquisite saris, served us at the table but did not sit down and eat with us. They did not join us in the sitting room either. It seemed to me they were being treated like exotic servants and not family. I found out later that this was the custom in high Indian society. I longed to get up and help with washing up but I could not do so. One had to accept their hospitality as it was given according to their culture.

Never underestimate what prayer can do.

In the city was an Assemblies of God Church. Part of their ministry was a counselling centre, and above the counselling rooms was a prayer room. It was always open for people to go and pray, or for people to go to ask for prayer for themselves. This prayer room was very peaceful. Across one wall was a mural of Jesus praying over Jerusalem with the words Jesus prayed written above, "O Jerusalem, Jerusalem . . . . how often I have longed to gather your children together, as a hen gathers her chicks under her wings, but you were not willing". They also had a twenty four hour telephone service, like the Samaritans in England.

One day as I was driving one of my African colleagues back from the township where she had been working she asked me if I would drive her to a chemist as she was not feeling very well. I glanced at her and realised she was in fact very ill, so at her further request I drove her to the African hospital in the city. I waited for her in the car and after a while a nurse came to tell me Brigalia had been admitted and that she was very ill indeed.

I returned to the hostel where, over the next few days, we prayed for Brigalia's recovery. Contact with the hospital informed us Brigalia was on the critical list, they did not think she was going to survive. One evening working in my office and thinking about Brigalia I learned a great lesson. As I prayed for her an inner voice told me to pick up the phone and ask for prayer at the prayer room at the Assemblies of God. I found myself arguing what difference would it make when we were praying for her anyway. The inner voice was persistent. I found myself compelled to pick up the phone and dial the number for the twenty four hour call centre. I explained why I had phoned and the person who answered said "Well let us pray together now". Pray over the phone, that is weird I thought. However, each of us prayed that God would lay His hand on Brigalia and heal her. The next day two of us went to see Brigalia. She was very weak but obviously a lot better. As I approached the bed Brigalia looked at me and said that an angel had visited her, and assured her she was going to get well. "Do you know when this was?" I asked her. "About nine o'clock". Then I realised this was the time I had phoned the call centre. I learned the powerful lesson, if God asked you to do something and you know for certain it is God, don't argue, obey.

About a year ago I was sent a newspaper cutting with a picture of Brigalia. She is now in a high position in the social services in South Africa. I was so happy to see that she had found a good position to serve her country.

One morning on my way to the market with Joseph I began to feel unwell. I felt as if I had a dose of flu coming on. By the time we returned to the hostel I had to retire to bed. My head was pounding, my whole body was hurting, and it became difficult for me to breath. Realising I had developed a very high temperature I called the doctor who thought I had got a severe dose of flu. Over the next few days my temperature rose higher. I could not eat, my breathing was harsh and I could not lie down flat because of severe pain in my chest and back. The doctor returned a few times over the next two weeks. My temperature fluctuated between 102-104 degrees. When I recovered I was told that that when people came to see how I was getting on I just talked a lot of rubbish, the fever had obviously made me very confused. Then one night as I tried to get out of bed I blacked out. By this time Frances was sleeping in the flat to look after me (not allowed under the Apartheid rules!). The doctor came in the morning and I was taken to hospital where I remained for a month. I was suffering from viral pneumonia. It was only then I found out that Durban and that part of the coast was known as pneumonia coast. The humidity was so high anyone with a respiratory weakness was liable to go down with pneumonia. Because I had had T.B. The doctors were particularly anxious I would succumb once more. However, the Vicar and a couple of others from the church family came and laid hands on me and prayed for my recovery. After one month I recovered. Because I had had several months of treatment in the T.B. Hospital with streptomycin it was difficult to find the right drug to deal with the pneumonia. When I got home, as advised by the doctors I went away for a month, and stayed at a lovely Christian Hotel on the border of Basutoland.

I returned to the Hostel expecting this to be my life's work. It was not to be. After a while I began suffering from serious throat infections. I had a lot of treatment but ended up having to have my tonsils and adenoids removed. This again was because of the humid climate. I was then told by the consultant I could no longer live in the Natal climate and Durban in particular. Because of this the next step along the way God was leading me began.

Chapter 10

Back to England

1961-1962

It all came as a bit of a blow. I thought the rest of my working life would be as the warden of the Y.W.C.A. I was very happy there, I had several friends, I belonged to a very good Church Fellowship. I was thirty one years old and I felt fulfilled.

"You must consider moving to a different climate", the specialist who performed my throat operation told me. He suggested I should return to the Cape Province. It was a time of much heart searching. Where could I go? What could I do? It wasn't as if I had a home to go to. I did not have another job to go to. My Vicar, Harold Wallwork, and his wife Mabel invited me to their home for tea one Sunday afternoon. They discussed some ideas with me. I had a desire to have some deeper teaching about the scriptures. There was a Bible School on the coast in the Cape Province. Enquiries were made; however, I could not go there. I had no school leaving certificate; these were required. What about training as a missionary? This was no good, it was too risky for someone like me. The illnesses I had suffered made me a risk for training as a missionary.

"Have you ever thought of going back to England?" I said I had not done so. I was a naturalised South African. South Africa was my adopted country. I had no contacts in England except the friend mentioned in chapter three with the two children with cerebral palsy.

About two weeks later I went to visit Peggie and Edward. Peggie was one of the Wardens at the Cape Town Y.W.C.A. who had shown me such Christ-like love and was the person who influenced me to give my life to Christ. They lived only twelve miles away. They had moved to Natal a few years earlier; they were both aware of my present situation. While we were having tea Peggie said, "Have you ever thought of returning to England?" I was a bit taken aback, "You must have been talking to Harold and Mabel." "We have not seen them for months", Peggie replied. It was at this point we realised that God was saying something. Harold and Mabel, Peggie and Edward, and myself of course began to ask the Holy Spirit to guide me into the path I should take.

Harold made the suggestion it might be possible for me to go to theological college in England. They were on the point of deciding that they should return to England for the sake of their third child who was profoundly deaf. If he was to finish his education in South Africa he would have to go to a special school for the deaf a thousand miles away from Durban. If they returned to England he could go to a special school for the deaf and still be reasonably near to home. As they prayed about their own situation, it became clear that it was right for them to return to England. When they knew they were definitely returning and where they would be, they told me that if I was accepted to train at a theological college then their home would be mine as well for the duration of my training.

The more I prayed it became clear that I should return to England. There were many details to be sorted out. What would I be training for? Harold was so helpful. "You can train as a Parish Worker. At the end of your training, when you are accepted, you would become part of the staff at a parish church." In those early days there was no thought of women becoming ordained as deacon or priest. After two years in a parish, if a woman felt God was calling her to do so she could be ordained into the diaconate and become a deaconess, but that was the end of the line.

The more I prayed about the whole situation and read the scriptures, the desire to follow the path of training for church work became stronger. The Lord graciously gave me a verse to hold on to: "You have not chosen me, but I have chosen you that you should go forth and bear fruit and that fruit shall remain". That verse came up several times along my journey, sometimes as positive encouragement that God wanted me to follow the path of ministry in the church and sometimes when I met opposition in one way or another. So began the next phase of my life's journey, both physical and spiritual. My desire to serve, my faith, my trust in God's provision was to be tried more than once; I found myself questioning if I was right: was I following God's will for me? Is this really the way God wants me to go?

The Passport and the Passage

I did not have a passport and had to apply for one. When my family sailed to South Africa in 1946, I was underage and was included on my mother's passport. When I made the application for my own passport I discovered I needed a birth certificate which I did not have. I wrote to Somerset House in London only to discover my birth was not registered. I contacted my Mother now living in my eldest brother's home. She confirmed that my birth had not been registered. On the advice of Harold Wallwork I consulted a solicitor who advised me to go to a solicitor with my mother. She would have to sign an affidavit that I was her child and confirm the place and date of my birth. I made the journey to Cape Town to get this done. To say my mother was not best pleased was putting it mildly!! I was so grateful that on the day appointed for this to take place mother was sober. What a relief! It made the verbal abuse that came later much easier to take. Hurdle number one was over as far as the passport was concerned.

Next came the arrangements for a passage back to England. I began to look for the cheapest way I could travel. The cheapest but complicated way was to sail to Italy, from there across to France, then across the channel to Dover I did not relish the thought of travelling in that way, as well as coping with all my luggage. Thankfully for me, friends advised me to travel from Southampton to London, then from there to Aylesbury and we drove to Grendon Underwood. Harold Wallwork had been instituted as vicar at Grendon Underwood. Harold and Mabel offered me a room to stay in until I went to college and during the vacations until I completed my training. I owe them a great deal. At the time of writing this book they have both died.

After Harold died Mabel returned up north, to her original home town. By this time their eldest daughter had married and moved away. Their profoundly deaf son finished his education. He became independent, had his own flat and worked for one of the large supermarkets.

The YMCA Warden

"Goodbye".
On board the "Caernarfon Castle"

I made several enquiries about a passage by ship to England. The cheapest fare I could find was on the Union Castle Line. The Caernarfon Castle was sailing on its last voyage between South Africa and England before it was decommissioned.

Happy I had found a passage I now had to work out how I was going to pay for it. I did not have a lot of money. I did not earn a large salary. For a couple of years I was no longer having to send money to my brother Rex to help support my mother so I had been putting money into a savings account, however this would not cover all I needed to meet my expenses. I had two items of furniture which were my own (the staff flat was furnished); I sold my radiogram and rather nice bookcase. This money would not cover my fare. The deposit for my fare had to be paid two months before my departure. Doubts began to creep in. Am I right? Is this really what I am meant to be doing? Am I in God's will? Am I following my own desires? I talked it over with my colleague Eve. She encouraged me by telling me she was sure I was doing what God intended.

I was getting near the day for the deposit to be paid on my passage. I returned to the hostel one afternoon and found a letter on the residents' letter rack addressed to me. I opened it to find a cheque inside for the exact amount needed to pay for the deposit on my fare. There was a note inside telling me what the money was for. I did not know the person who sent it. "My God will supply every need of yours according to His riches in glory in Christ Jesus" (the Revised Standard Version). As soon as I could I cashed the cheque and took the money to the shipping office.

In the months before my departure I received various amounts of money which I placed in the Post Office. When I arrived in England I had forty eight pounds to my name. It does not sound much now, however I was very grateful to have it. Friends gave me several items of clothing for both summer and winter. This was marvellous and kept me well clothed until I was in my first parish. One friend gave me a wonderful winter overcoat. How grateful I was for that coat. My first year in college (1963) was a very cold winter indeed, especially for someone who had come from such a hot and humid area in South Africa.

The day the Caernarfon Castle sailed from Durban I had to be on board mid-morning. Throughout the day many people came to bid me farewell. It was rather an emotional time. I have a lovely memory of being handed a large sealed envelope with the instruction "Do not open until tomorrow." When I opened the envelope I found twenty one letters, one for each day until I reached Southampton; twenty one friends had each written a letter to cheer me on my way and encourage me as I entered into the next phase of my life. Each letter was such a blessing.

So began my three week journey. I looked upon this time as a holiday. The ship docked at East London, Port Elizabeth and Cape Town before the final two week journey to Southampton. At each port a few friends came to bid me farewell. As the ship docked for four days in Cape Town I was able to go to say goodbye to my eldest brother Rex and my mother. My mother told me she could not understand what I was doing but wished me well in the best way she could. As promised I kept in touch with my mother until some years later when she died while I was in my first Parish. I did not see my brother Austin; at that time no one knew where he was.

As we sailed from Cape Town I came across a missionary couple I had met a few times. They were returning to England on furlough. We discovered we had been invited to dine at the Captain's table each evening until we reached Southampton, we were so surprised, but really enjoyed ourselves, until we reached the Bay of Biscay when it became very stormy. We spent each evening playing scrabble with the first officer. We felt really privileged and special!

So I reached the land of my birth. "What was in front of me?" I wondered.

Chapter 11

Theological College

1962-1964

The ship arrived at Southampton. I leaned on the rails and watched as two tugs manoeuvred the ship into its berth. It was a typical cold and dull winter's day in February. I was so thankful for that lovely winter coat I had been given.

The passengers all disembarked and eventually I was reunited with my luggage (a tin trunk, three suitcases and a sewing machine); the latter I had brought for its owner who had returned to England months previously. I really cannot remember how I managed it but I got a train to London, then another train to Aylesbury where I was met by Harold Wallwork. It must have been quite a journey as all my luggage went with me. There were still railway porters in those days!

Here I was back in England. It felt like arriving in a foreign country. I was sixteen years old when as a family we sailed to South Africa; now here I was at thirty two and having to readjust to the country of my birth.

I settled down in Harold and Mabel's vicarage which was in the village of Grendon Underwood. Things began to happen quickly; I had to find a job to support myself. I applied for three areas of employment, one of which was in London with the Scripture Union book shop. I was unsuccessful. In the meantime Harold had made an appointment for me to see the Bishop of Buckingham with a view to me becoming a Parish Worker. The Bishop was very kind. Two things stand out about that interview. The first was he told me he was amazed I had travelled seven thousand miles with so little money and no assurance at that point that I would be accepted for training. He said he recognised I had a strong faith. Secondly he offered me a job. "Are you willing to accept any employment?" he asked. When I replied that I was, he went on to tell me he was guardian to an elderly aristocratic lady, a spinster, who after the death of her sister was looking for a companion help. "She will not be easy and is rather demanding", he warned me. If I agreed to take this post I would receive board and lodging and a salary of sixteen pounds per month. As it was only for eight months (I hoped to be in college by then) I was willing to have a go. The Bishop assured me that if it got too difficult for me he would make other arrangements. I stayed with Miss Hethketh the whole eight months. She was not easy to look after! The Bishop came to visit her every couple of weeks. Then when he had to go overseas for a couple of months she took to her bed and became a self imposed invalid. I cooked all her favourite food and in the evenings I read to her. "Born Free" was the first book I read. She really enjoyed the story of Elsa the lioness. As soon as the Bishop returned she got up out of bed and resumed her life as before! I am sure she looked on him as a son; she really adored him.

Looking after Miss Hethketh was very helpful to me not only because it gave me a salary, but because by this time I had been advised to do a course of English in advance of attending a Selection Conference. Also, the powers that be insisted I go to see an education Psychologist. They were very worried because my schooling had ended at the age of thirteen and a half. They felt I would not be able to cope with a theological training. In answer to their many questions I could only say to them "I know God has called me to do this. If this is His will He will enable me to cope with study". I had enough time to study while looking after Miss Hethketh.

I had my interview with the educational Psychologist. Somewhere over the years I have lost the copy of the letter she wrote with her assessment of my abilities. However I remember some of her remarks. One was: she said I had such perseverance and determination I would be able to make up any loss of education in my two years at theological college. The second remark which gave me and the Wallworks such amusement was, "Helen's intelligence is better than 50% of the population". We laughed so much and wondered what was wrong with 50% of the population?

Next came the selection conference. This became a real test of my faith and God's call. There were four selectors. These people are chosen because of their ability in this area: the assessment of each candidate to see if they are suitable or not. Is their calling genuine? Do they have the abilities needed for ministry in the Church? There were four people who interviewed those of us who were at the selection conference. One of the selectors was a Vicar who I already knew. The interview with Martin Parsons was very pleasant and enjoyable. The other three were a great deal more probing especially on what experience I had of any church work in South Africa. It was the last interview that really threw me. For about three quarters of an hour this lady really knocked down any confidence I may have had about doing a theological college course; in her favour I need to explain she knew what she was talking about. She was an educationalist and an ex missionary. "You have not done enough reading since you left school." She meant I had not done the right kind of reading. I had read a great deal. I had not read theological books or allied subjects. "How do you ever hope to cope with lectures?" "How will you manage to write essays?" "How will you manage to cope with exams?" It seemed to me the questions would never end. I don't remember everything she said to me. However, I came away from that interview quite discouraged and convinced I would not be selected. As I stood outside her door I was suddenly overwhelmed with resentment, anger and bitterness against my parents. I was not knowingly aware that I carried these feelings; I did know it was wrong. I ran up the stairs to my room and poured out my heart to God. "O Lord, I cannot keep these feelings in my heart, it will not hurt anyone but myself. Please forgive me and take these feelings away. If I have misread Your will about my training and serving You in the church please show me". Needing some spiritual comfort I opened my "Daily Light" (this is a book of daily readings for morning and evening, all from the Bible). I turned to July 3rd: how good is our God. The words on the page for the evening of that day were God speaking to me directly. Here are just a few of the verses, "Now when they saw the boldness of Peter and John, and perceived that they were uneducated, common men, they wondered; and recognised that they had been with Jesus", "God chose what is low and despised in the world", "My speech and my message were not in plausible words of wisdom, but in demonstration of the Spirit and power, that your faith might not rest in the wisdom of men but in the power of God", and the verse I had in South Africa encouraging me to go ahead: "You did not choose me, but I chose you and appointed you that you should go and bear fruit, for apart from me you can do nothing". All the verses on that page spoke to me and my situation. I thanked my Heavenly Father for His assurance, for a new peace in my heart and went back from the selection conference to wait. A short while later I found I had been passed as suitable for a theological training.

It was about a year later at St. Michael's College in Oxford I met Miss Turner. She was the person appointed by the Diocese to look after the women who were in training for parish work. She took me aside and after finding out how I was getting on she said, "You know at the selection conference we sat up until one o'clock in the morning discussing your case. We realised you had a lot of experience with people, but academically we did not think you were suitable, but then something urged us to let you through". In my heart I said it was not something but Someone. I felt it would be insolent to have expressed that to her directly. However, it was good of her to have told me. I did finish my two years at St. Michael's House in Oxford. St. Michael's House became, with three other colleges, Trinity College Bristol; we were very glad about this.

I valued my time at college, I valued the whole experience, the teaching, the fellowship. The discipline was valuable (though some of it was sometimes over the top for someone my age) and stood me in good stead in the years of my ministry. In my second year I was made vice senior student.

I was so grateful to those who taught us, those who were our lecturers. The Revd. Basil Gough, who at the time was the Rector of St. Ebbes Church in the city, was our chaplain and also lectured us on pastoral studies. The Revd. Jim Spence, senior Curate at St. Ebbes, gave us lectures on doctrine and the prayer book. I am quite convinced I passed my doctrine and prayer book exams because of his clear teaching. Then there was Deaconess Tatton who lectured us on pastoralia, or as it became half way through our studies: "The Christian in Contemporary Society".

I was fortunate to have two grants to cover my fees. I earned a little money in the vacations; for two Christmases a fellow student and myself worked at the Post Office. The first year sorting letters, the second year sorting parcels. We did twelve hour shifts. At the end of our time we were glad to get home to sleep and rest. We did earn a decent amount of money which was a great help.

Misdemeanours at College

Because many of us were older women who had held down responsible jobs before entering theological college, we were a bit disconcerted to find we were treated a bit like sixth formers at school; it was a rule that we were in college by nine o'clock at night unless we had a pass to stay out later. My first misdemeanour was to still have someone in college after nine o'clock, even though it was only five past nine as my visitor left! I was just seeing Jean Savage out of the door when the principal came in and I was in trouble. I was given a severe dressing down for breaking this rule and reminded that nobody should be out after nine and no visitors should still in the building after nine. Each weekend everything we needed for a light evening meal was left out for us by the housekeeper. One weekend she forgot to put out the bread. Being a practical person I went to the pantry to fetch the bread. It did not seem right to me to fetch the housekeeper from the top of the house where she lived. We all knew where everything was kept. The next day I was in deep trouble for taking it upon myself to do such a thing! Naughty me!!

St. Michael's House. Faculty and students.
Me second row, third from right.

I think my worst sin was when I omitted to wear a hat when I went to London for an interview with the possibility of becoming a Parish Worker in that particular church. When I returned to college I was summoned by our Deaconess; she told me how disappointed she was in me. This was my second year in college and I had been made a vice senior student. This made it far worse in Deaconess Tatton's eyes. I suspected this was not the end of the matter. Sure enough the next day at lunch the principal stood up and we all had a lecture about the times in life when one should wear a hat! I don't think the Vicars of the parishes where we went to serve would worry one way or the other. I am afraid we found it all rather silly and had a good laugh about it. Thank God for a sense of humour!

We were so glad when the women's colleges and the men's colleges joined together and everything became more balanced.

Towards the end of our time at St. Michael's House the sister of the then Archbishop of Canterbury, Norah Coggan, came to speak to those of us who were training to become Parish Workers. She urged us to become the best we could in our learning and spirituality because she felt the day would come when we would be ordained into the full orders of the Church. Before we left to go to our respective parishes our principal said the same thing to us. I think those women had a real vision of the future.

After my third interview, which was with the Vicar of St. Jude's in Plymouth and subject to the approval of the Bishop of Exeter, I was to begin my ministry in the autumn of 1964.

CHAPTER 12

My First Parish

While still at Theological College, students who were training for parochial work began to search for the right church to begin their ministry as "Parish Worker" or "Lady Worker". I don't think any of us liked the title very much! Yet that is what we were in those days.

How does one know, what guidance does one have to know that this is where God means you to be? I can only answer for myself. I had already been to a few churches in the London area for interviews; none of these proved to be the right place. I was constantly praying, asking that I be guided to the right parish. I did not want to be out of God's will for me. Eventually, the principal of St. Michael's House told me about St. Jude's in Plymouth. They had a Lady Worker who was moving on. The Revd. Peter Pytches was the Vicar; this was his first living. St. Jude's had a Curate and now Peter was looking for a Lady Worker to make up the team.

I travelled to Plymouth for an interview; it was agreed I would stay at the vicarage for the week-end. Arriving at the Vicarage I was met by Beryl (Peter's wife) and two very lively and friendly boys, Paul four and a half years old and Andrew two and a half years old. All these years later there a few things that remain in one's memory. Over the week-end Paul and Andrew came down the stairs singing "Aunty Helen is a melon, Aunty Helen is a melon"; this I thought to myself is acceptance. I love children, so I appreciated the fact they had taken to me.

There was the warmth of the welcome Peter and Beryl gave me. I appreciated Peter's straightforwardness about what he expected from a woman colleague.

All these years later when we are together (I visit them at least once a year) we still laugh when we remember how Peter said to me, "I don't mind what you wear, as long as it is not a green suit!!" St. Michael's expected or had expected all lady workers going into parishes to wear a standard suit of mottled green. Peter did not know that these suits were not being worn anymore; my predecessor wore hers all the time! We students in my time of training were so glad about this, they really were ghastly and quite frumpish.

Both Peter and Beryl have a lovely sense of humour, "Would you like a bath?" they asked as we were about to retire for the night?!! Funnily enough when I went for the last interview for my second Parish the Vicar and his wife asked me the same question; I desperately wanted to laugh but did not dare to do so.

Dick Mulrenan and his wife did have a sense of humour but they were very seriously minded and would not have found the question funny even if I was able to explain.

Over that week-end in Plymouth as I sat in church on the Sunday morning I was suddenly overcome with the feeling: 'I have been here before, it feels like home.' I had never been to Plymouth before and certainly not to St. Jude's! Together with being with the family, seeing round the parish, speaking with Peter at length, and now this! I was becoming aware this was where I was meant to be. At the end of that week-end Peter said he felt we could work together; I felt the same way, we prayed together and I returned to college. Peter said he would let me know if I was to become St. Jude's Lady Worker or not as soon as he could.

Things do not always go as smoothly as we hope they will. A mistake was made, sadly by my college.

A notice was put into the Church Newspapers about which parish we Lady Workers were going to. Peter phoned me, he was distressed about this; he naturally thought I had given the information about my own appointment. I had not done so. Peter had to say he could not commit himself to me being appointed as a member of staff before the Bishop had given his consent. However, it did work out in the end and I did become the next Lady Worker at St. Jude's.

I began my ministry there in October 1964. I was welcomed into the parish on my first Sunday there; I was officially licensed as a Lady Worker by the then Bishop of Plymouth, Guy Sanderson, on the 27th March 1966. I was working while I waited for this!

Before I left St. Michael's House I failed one of the exams. It was a subject that had been changed half way through our studies. Pastoralia was changed to bring it up to date. It became "The Christian in Contemporary Society". The exam covered a wide spectrum of society. The aim was to be able to bring a Christian mind to all areas of society. Even students at St. Michael's far more able than myself, and even those with degrees, failed as well. I had to re-sit this exam in my first year in the parish.

Peter was a great help in advising me how to approach the exam as was a nurse who was a member of the congregation. One of the areas of knowledge one needed was to be able to show that you were aware of how people with psychiatric and allied problems could be helped to live in society and not have to remain in hospital or institutions for the rest of their lives. The nurse who helped me with this was herself nursing in these specialised areas. She was able to give me a great deal of literature to study. With this help, and the fact that a question in the exam was on this very subject, I passed the exam. What a relief!

In the early days of women in the ministry, accommodation was not provided by the church. I had obtained two rooms at the top of a town house a few blocks down the hill from the vicarage. My landlady, Mrs. Brookshaw, was a kindly soul. She was also very nosey and wanted to know all about each person who came to see me. I had to be firm with her and tried to explain to her that in my position as a church minister I could not do as she wished. I stayed there for nine of my ten years in Plymouth. In my last year there I was offered a flat very near to the church, which was very helpful.

Main Ministry

The main focus of my ministry in those early days was the children. There were two Sunday Schools, one in the morning for the children from the upper part of the parish, and in the afternoon for the children from the lower part of the parish. It was thought it would be sensible to amalgamate the two. This became my responsibility; it did take place after a period of time, it was not an easy task, but eventually it was successfully achieved.

There were four women's meetings. I became the leader of two of these, the Women's Fellowship and the LHMU (Ladies Home Mission Union), which was a branch of the Church Pastoral Aid Society. CPAS is an Evangelical Home Mission caring for the needs of the incumbents and their staff all over the country. I was the recipient of one of the grants they gave for training. I also received a grant from them towards my salary.

Beryl, Peter's wife, led the Young wives group called "Homemakers", she also led the Mothers Union meetings. Beryl also set up a very valuable ministry of a Play Group. This group met once a week to encourage mothers with their very young children to come and meet together in a warm and friendly atmosphere. Over tea, coffee and biscuits (the children had squash), the mums were able to chat to one another and discuss any problems, if they had any. There was a variety of toys for the children to play with.

The mothers and their children, and hopefully husbands, would be encouraged to come to the monthly family services; quite a few did but not all.

When the children reached four years old they were encouraged to come into the Sunday school. Sunday schools had changed a great deal in the 1960's. There were varied visual aids, lots of activity, and acting out of biblical stories. We benefited from lesson outlines from the CPAS and other sources. When the children reached seven years old they moved to junior Sunday School (Explorers). St. Jude's had entered the Pathfinder Movement. Explorers was the junior section of the organisation. All the children from four years to seven years were my responsibility.

I really enjoyed this ministry. I did quite a bit of study on the teaching of children and how they learn. I had several junior teachers and it was my responsibility to teach them how to teach. I introduced some older women into the Sunday school. They sat with the children during the teaching time. They helped them as they arrived with their hats and coats and when they went home. They became surrogate grannies. The children bonded with them. We found this made for good behaviour.

At eleven years old the children became Pathfinders, the older section of the Pathfinder Organisation already mentioned. Eventually, the fifteen and over young people entered CYFA. This was good: every child and young person in the church belonged and benefited from all that the organisation provided. The Curate had responsibility for this older group.

On Sunday evenings after church the young people got together for what was called "Sunday Squash". This was time of general chat and discussion. The Curate and myself were always in attendance. It was not a formal meeting but more a time of relaxation.

Friday night was youth club night with all kinds of activity: games, music, and table tennis. In the summer they would go out for various activities. We had a lovely group of young people for which we were really grateful. I can still remember how they wanted to reach out to other young people who never came to church. After discussion it was agreed we should let them have a go. They did their best but after a while they had to agree it did not work. They were trying to cope with young people who were quite rough, and they realised they could not handle the situation.

The Explorers had a mid-week club which I ran. We were fortunate in having two church halls. In the winter months I organised games and other activities in the lower hall. Sometimes I had the help of a young man who would play five-aside football with the boys in the top hall. On one occasion these boys taught me a child's sense of justice. One afternoon two boys came down to the lower hall rather angry. They told me that Robert (not his real name) was a cheat and far too bossy. "If he stays we will not come any more," they said. The children were right and I had a dilemma on my hands. I explained to Robert as best I could. To my relief he informed me he wanted to give up. Robert was a very self assured young man. I met him quite some years later when I was on holiday and paid a visit to St. Jude's. It was good to see him still part of the church Fellowship. He was now a business man in his own right, married and with children of his own.

In the summer we went out. One club day I had arranged to take the seven to elevens to Paignton Zoo. The morning of the outing my two leaders let me know they were not able to come. I then made the decision to cope with the children on my own. When we arrived at the zoo I told the children (there was twenty of them) that if they did not stay close to me all the time, there would be trouble. They were extremely well behaved (much to my relief!), however, there was a very funny incident. The children knew I had come from South Africa; as we made our way round looking at the various animals we came to the tropical bird section. In the enclosure in front of us there was a very large African Stork. When it suddenly gave out a very loud squawking noise, with great glee, a few of the children said, "Wow! Miss Lawrence he recognises you!!" There was great laughter all round.

After the evening service on Sundays at the Squash, we sometimes had a discussion on a topic that was relevant to the teenagers. One evening we had a discussion on "Discipline in the Home". We asked them what they did if Mum or Dad insisted on them being at home at night by a certain time. Their answer amazed us. "We don't like it, we think we are old enough to stay out longer than they wish. We may argue against their decision but we know they do this because they love and care for us. So we do as they say". That was the early 1960's. I wonder how youngsters today would answer that question?

The Curate and myself introduced the idea of the eleven to fifteen year old young people going away to summer camps and house parties. The Church Pastoral Aid Society ran these every year. It meant I would go as a Leader and take a group of girls from the Parish with me. The curate would do the same with the boys. We approached the parents and explained to them what it was all about. It was a very new idea; some of the parents were very insular, they had never travelled any further than Exeter. London or elsewhere in the country would have been like a foreign country to them.

We did convince the parents what a good thing it would be for their children to have this experience. For the rest of my time at St. Jude's in most years I did take a group of the girls to a house party. I became one of the leaders. The youngsters really did enjoy themselves and came home full of enthusiasm. It was a time of adventure for them. They mixed with young people from all over the country. The House Party usually lasted for one week during which they were taken on outings or played outdoor games. There were several indoor games; we were in school property which meant we had a large hall to organise games in if the weather was not good.

After the evening meal there was a meeting during which they sang, learning new songs and hymns. One of the leaders would give a talk on a biblical theme. After an evening milky drink it was time for bed. Tired though the young people were the leaders had the job of getting them to settle! This became a valuable time as each leader could comfort anyone who might be homesick, or listen to their problems. These were great days; it was a joy to see many of these young people develop spiritually and come into a personal relationship with God. Each leader of a group or dormitory had the responsibility to put the young people in touch with the minister of their local church in their home town. We hoped they would be cared for spiritually. Some of them did come from difficult homes, and they needed support. The leaders also kept in touch by letter.

A few days after Christmas the Curate and myself, with a few people from the congregation, took the eleven to fifteen years old Pathfinders to a Youth Adventure centre on Dartmoor, just outside Prince Town and not all that far from Dartmoor Prison! An army youth team supplied us with activities: archery, trampolines, snooker and table tennis. We took plenty of indoor games in case of bad weather.

The Centre was wonderfully set up. The only hardship I can remember was the intense cold. Getting into one's bunk at night, brrrh! It took ages to warm up. We had great rambles over the moors and came back very hungry. Those of us who did the cooking had this in hand. I had obtained a recipe for a dish called "seven layer dinner", it was so popular the young people requested we had this each year. It was basically every vegetable you could get hold of in layers in the dish, with rice in between the layers, sausages all over the top and condensed tomato soup poured all over, very tasty and quite filling. Even youngsters who might be fussy loved it!

The one thing we had to do before we went was to contact the weather centre. Dartmoor can be very treacherous and especially so at that time of the year. Needless to say our adventurous young people thought it might be fun to be cut off on the moors! It only happened one year when we had to cancel at the last minute because it was too risky. The youngsters were so disappointed, we had to explain we were responsible for their safety. I think they forgave us!

Two Amusing Occasions

Once at one of the house parties as a leader I was asked to accompany a group of girls to some horse riding stables. That day there was no other leader available. When we arrived at the stables, the horses were brought out for the girls and I was asked "was I going to ride?" I explained I had never ridden and would not know what to do. "As you are here you really should ride as well. Don't worry we have a very gentle horse you can ride." As they led out the horse I was to ride, I gulped. It was a beautiful dappled grey horse. However it looked so high, I could not imagine myself getting up on it let alone riding it!! The owners saw the look on my face, "Come on now stop worrying, we will help you up and will tell you what to do". It turned out to be a most enjoyable experience. Led by one person we rode out into the countryside and after a while of walking we were instructed (at least I was) to get the horses to trot, "Now don't sit stiffly in the saddle, but go with the movement of the horse". At the end of that morning, I realised that I had got the bug for horse riding. I resolved that when I got back to the parish I would seek out some stables and on my day off would go and have some riding lessons. It never came to pass; I had no idea how expensive it would be. Sadly I have never been on a horse since.

Another year at one of the house parties I was asked to accompany a group of girls all between eleven years old and fifteen on a trip to France for the day. I refused on the grounds I could not speak French. I was told I had to go as I was the only older responsible leader left that day. I was given one of the younger leaders to accompany me. We crossed the channel on the ferry and arrived at Calais. As the girls were hungry we made our way towards the town to buy some fish and chips. We had not gone far when we were pursued by a group of older teenage boys. I was not too worried to begin with. Then these boys began to tease the older girls, they in turn began to get very nervous. How do you tell someone in French to "go away"? I then got my junior leader to get the younger girls round her, and I got the older girls round me. We coped at the fish and chip shop and I thought the boys had gone away. The girls then wanted to go to a nearby fair. Oh dear! The boys arrived there also. This time they were determined to get the older girls to go with them; I then asked the girls if any of them learnt French at school. Two of them said "yes". How do you tell someone to "go away" "leave us alone"? They told me what they thought were the right words; I tried it out, unfortunately it was incorrect. Obviously the boys thought this was very funny and renewed their efforts. Now the girls were really upset and began to cry. I resorted to gesticulating and eventually they moved off. I had now had enough and said to everyone, "Come on we are going back to the ferry".

We made our way back and as we approached the entrance to the docks, to my dismay back came the French boys. Now they ran up to the girls and tried to put their arms round them. That was too much, I needed help, I saw a man whom I thought may be some dockyard official; unfortunately he could not understand English. He could however see the situation and tried to get the boys to go away; at this point they all ran up some steel girders and down the other side to get back to the girls again. It was then I noticed an Auto mobile Association kiosk, so getting the girls altogether in a huddle, I went into the kiosk and asked if anyone could speak English. They did, so I explained the situation to them and asked them if they would call a Gendarme. Very soon a Gendarme arrived and dealt with the boys and got them to go away. He came back to me and apologised in English; "I am very sorry this happened to you in my country, I hope it will not stop you from coming again". When we arrived back at the house party my first words were "Don't you ever ask me to do anything like that again." I was exhausted. Looking back at it afterwards I could see how in one sense it was funny, but not while I was dealing with it!

During the years I was at St. Jude's it became known as a Parish who sent people out to serve Christ. There were those who became Clergymen, a certain number became overseas missionaries and quite a few of them are now retired but still serving God in their retirement.

CHAPTER 13

Limitation of early ministry

1964-1974

I really enjoyed my ministry with the children as well as the leadership of the two women's meetings. Visiting in the parish was important, quite a few afternoons would see me out visiting, maybe, parishioners who were ill or those who were elderly and housebound; sometimes it would be someone who had been a church member and no longer came for one reason or another. Two hospitals were very near; I visited the hospitals as well, especially members of our own congregation.

An area of ministry I did not expect came my way. A very short service was broadcast to the hospitals.

This was done in the early evening and the patients could tune in on their bedside radios. It was a bit of a learning curve for me. It was quite an old system, and I realise how much more up to date it would be now! We had to prepare our own short service and then broadcast it. It was encouraging when someone told us how helpful they had found it.

I was called to speak at women's meetings quite frequently all around the city in the various denominations. There were some amusing moments at these meetings. I arrived to be greeted by the leader, "You have come prepared to sing a solo haven't you"; alarmed I replied "No I'm afraid I haven't I have only come to speak". "Your predecessor always sang a solo when she came, so you will sing for us won't you, please?" I had to do some quick thinking, I grabbed hold of a hymn book and in a bit of a panic I found a gospel song I knew from my days in South Africa. When the time came for me to sing I was handed a microphone, help! It was bad enough to have to sing but to use a mike as well! I sent up a quick arrow prayer and plunged in as it were. The group of ladies were so pleased, I was exhausted! Later when I was at the Vicarage and shared this incident with Peter and Beryl we saw the funny side of it all and had a great laugh.

On another occasion in a different church there was a lady at the meeting who was a bit "disturbed"; she interrupted the meeting several times. At the end she approached me in anger and said "who do you think you are—Lord Beecham?" As my talk had nothing to do with railways I think I just stood and let her carry on her tirade.

Limitations of a Lady Worker

Although I was fully trained to lead services and to preach I could only begin my ministry as a Lay Worker. Therefore, there were areas of ministry I could not enter into. It was frustrating in a sense, but like many other women in those early days I carried on with what I was able to do. At St. Jude's we had a monthly family service. Because this was not an authorised service I was able to speak at it and lead it, which I did now and again. Several of my fellow students at St. Michael's House were so frustrated by the situation; they went into other areas of ministry, while others returned to their original areas of work. I was content to stay in parochial ministry knowing in my heart this was what God had called me to.

1972 Now a Deaconess

During the following years there was constant discussion taking place about the ordination of women. Sometimes what was said or broadcast in the media was very hurtful and some people in church circles and outside had very strong feelings about women being ordained. Some of my fellow women ministers were quite militant about the whole situation. I may have been wrong but I felt strongly that I was called into ministry to serve other people, not to fight my corner or my position in the Church. Even after two years when I could have applied to be ordained as a Deaconess I did not do so immediately. As I thought about it and prayed I decided to find out why and how some women had taken this step.

As I met some Deaconesses at quiet days and conferences and asked them why they made the decision I received different replies. "I was ordained as Deaconess to give me greater status". "I became a Deaconess so that I would have security". I knew that was not the way for me. Personally I was not in the ministry for status or security, but simply because I knew this was where God had led me so far. I decided to discuss this with two people in St. Jude's congregation. Jack and Joyce Barley were both very spiritually wise people. Jack was a licensed Reader at St. Jude's, Joyce was involved in many areas in the church. After discussion and prayer together we all felt the time was not right for me.

Some years later when I was wondering what God intended for me, and the issue of women being ordained was quite tense, some of my friends felt strongly that I should consider coming out of the ministry. They explained they did not feel there was any future for women in the ministry even if they had been ordained as a Deaconess. It was at that time that I was invited with the local clergy to the installation of a vicar at a nearby parish. As we were putting on our robes ready for the service I felt a hand on my shoulder and I turned to find it was Jack Barley; "Helen the time has come for you to put yourself forward to be ordained as a Deaconess". "But Jack you know the reason I have not done so", I replied. "Yes, I know" Jack said, "I feel God is saying the time is right now. I think you should be praying about it again". Respecting Jack as a spiritual and wise man I took his advice. Some weeks later I do remember as I prayed I said "I do not want to be out of your will for me, please give me some indication from your Word that this is the way forward". I cannot remember now how long afterwards it was but as I turned to the evening reading in my "Daily Light" these words jumped out of the page: "the gifts and the call of God are irrevocable". Yes, that was the answer to my prayer; God had called me into the ministry. He had given me the gifts I needed. He did not go back on His Word or His calling, therefore I could not go back either. I had to go forward in His grace and in His strength. I contacted the necessary authorities and entered a short period of further training. I had to find three people who would vouch for me. Jack and Joyce were the obvious choice. Peter Pytches was no longer Vicar of St. Jude's by that time. David Lumb, who was now Vicar, was my second choice. A friend who had known me for some time was the third choice. My further training was to spend a month at the Royal Devon and Exeter Hospital as an assistant Chaplain. I was advised to go for a ministry I would choose if I was not in parochial ministry. I thoroughly enjoyed my month at the hospital ministering to patients in various wards. It was a valuable time of learning. I found patients were so grateful to have someone to talk to about their problems of ill health, how it was affecting them and their families. They were generally grateful when one offered to pray with them.

Before I was ordained as Deaconess, as instructed by the then Bishop of Plymouth, I had to go away to a convent in Devon for a one week retreat. I was the only person there on retreat: there were not many parochial workers in the Exeter Diocese. The whole time I was there the nuns did not speak to me. I ate my meals on my own. It was, however, a valuable time of study and prayer.

The day of my ordination as Deaconess was on the 31st March 1974. Little did I realise that by the end of that year I would be moving to serve in a new parish.

The still small voice at St. Jude's

I had already found that God will prompt one to go or to do something one was not thinking of doing at the time. This time it happened as I was returning home one afternoon from visiting. It was an unwritten rule in the parish that one did not visit a home after 4pm. This was the time the wife and mother cooked the evening meal. There were not too many working mums in those days. I was on my way home from visiting, walking up one of the hills (Plymouth is very hilly). I suddenly felt the impulse to go and visit one particular person. She was a mother in the poorer part of the parish. I glanced at my watch and said to myself, "I cannot go now it is past 4 o'clock". Again it was as if someone spoke to me. I did not hear an audible voice. I was convinced I had to go. I turned round and went down the hill and made my way to the home of the person mentioned. I arrived at the house and rang the bell, the mother came to the door looked at me and burst into tears, then told me she was wishing I would come. The reason for her distress was, she told me, her daughter was pregnant at fourteen from a relationship with a most unsuitable man. The daughter had the baby and with the support of her mother and father brought it up. As predicted the biological father did not want to take any responsibility for the baby. I do not know what happened to him. I am so glad I responded to that inner voice. This was not the first time I learned not to ignore that still small voice.

It was not long before I came to realise church families (congregations) are like any other families. There are many happy times, there are sad times. There are also times when members of the family disagree with one another, and also have to learn to forgive one another. We all have to learn to take on the teaching of Jesus. What about the ministers of the church? Speaking for myself, and looking back over the years, I realise there were situations I could have handled in a different way. I realise there were situations where I made mistakes; it is also true that we learn from our mistakes.

I had to learn not to hold on to grievances when someone had been hurtful in what they had said, or had accused me of saying or doing something I have not done at all. I usually found my peace, eventually, by taking the situation to the Lord and leaving it with Him.

On occasions over the years I was asked, "Do you find any opposition to women in the ministry?" The answer was "Yes, I do", however I recognised I was very fortunate as my ministry was accepted in the parishes where I worked. There were one or two people who held strong views about the ordination of women, and they would let me know how they felt. There was only one occasion I can remember during my time in Plymouth. One Bishop openly expressed his opinion that women would be responsible for bringing witchcraft in the Church! One other occasion after I was ordained as a Deaconess, I was invited to speak at a large women's meeting in Bournemouth. I was invited to lunch at the Vicarage. The Vicar had asked me what I did in my position as a Deaconess, when I told him he then said to me, "You do know don't you that you have gone against the ordinance of creation?" Somewhat taken aback I asked him what he meant. He then explained, "Adam was created first and then Eve, therefore women were inferior to men". He did not believe women could exercise the authority that comes with ordination. This made me very sad especially as he said he was thinking of looking for a woman colleague.

One person who expressed his feelings to me about the ordination of women was totally different. On my first Sunday after becoming the assistant curate at St. Michael's church in Braintree, as he met me at the church door he said, "I want you to know that I do not agree with the ordination of women". That was his opinion yet he never made a big issue of it. In all my years he never stayed away when I was leading a service or preaching, in fact there were times when I had preached he came to thank me, "Thank you Helen for that (meaning the passage I had preached on). I have never thought of that point like that". Here was a man who was so gracious in spite of the opinions he held; I had real respect for him.

Once I was really hurt when, at a particular clergy meeting after a discussion about women's ordination the speaker told us all "that women in the ministry were a threat to the men in the ministry"; one of my male colleagues took the speaker to task and said I was upset by his remarks. The speaker replied that I had misunderstood. My colleague came to me to tell me I had not misunderstood at all. After a short while I got over it. Life was too busy to go on holding on to hurts. I have always realised I was fortunate, I have not had as much to put up with as my fellow women in the ministry.

Goddaughters

When I had been at St. Jude's just over a year Peter and Beryl had their third child. As Beryl went into labour Peter brought Paul and Andrew to my flat and asked me to give them some breakfast (these are the boys mentioned in Chapter 12). When the baby was born Peter returned and invited me to go back to the Vicarage with them to see the baby, a girl. I entered the room and greeted Beryl, who sitting up in bed with the baby in her arms. It was then they asked me if I would become Godmother to Ruth. I felt really privileged; both Peter and Beryl come from large families, there were plenty of aunts and uncles. So Ruth became my first Godchild. I had the joy of seeing Ruth grow up. Ruth is married to Tim. They now live in Jersey and have two sons Alexander and Patrick. Tim works in a bank and Ruth is a teacher.

During my time at St. Jude's I became Godmother to another girl. This was Kate, short for Katherine. She was the second daughter of John and Isabel Young. John was the Curate at that time. Kate lives in York with her husband Jamie and their two children Emma and Jacob.

It was after I moved to Braintree in Essex as Assistant Curate that I was asked to become Godmother to Joanna. She was the second daughter of John and Doreen Bevin. John and Doreen were born and bred in Plymouth and were lifelong members of St. Jude's church, as were their respective parents. John was deputy head of one of the schools. Both John and Doreen were leaders in the church. I knew the family well. I was pleased to be asked to be Godmother to Joanna. Doreen died from Cancer. She was just able to go to Sarah's wedding (Johanna's eldest sister). John lived to see Joanna married, and to see his four grandchildren.

Joanna (now known as Jo) and her husband Mike are now living and working in Johannesburg, South Africa. Jo is a nurse and is nursing as well as looking after the family. After working in Devonport Dockyard Mike went into the Police Force. It was after Jo had been to Kenya to help with some building work for a charity that they both felt called to some specific work. They found that they were called to the Missionary Aviation Fellowship. Mike is at the time of writing Operations and Quality Manager and a Pilot for the MAF based in Johannesburg. I am very proud of them; they were first based in Chad but with other families they had to be evacuated because of the rebels coming over from Darfur. They returned safely to England. They had a time of recovery at their home in Devon and they are now based in Lanseria in Johannesburg. I am able to keep in touch with them via the Internet.

Colleagues while at St. Jude's

During the years I was at St. Jude's I worked with several curates. At the beginning of my ministry Ken Morris was the curate. He was married to Jane. Jane was a trained Psychologist. They were not able to have children. Eventually they made the decision to adopt. They adopted a lovely baby boy who they named Stefan. Stefan was of mixed race. He was a strikingly good looking child. About two years later they adopted a baby girl who was also of mixed race, they called her Bethan. Just after they had celebrated their tenth wedding anniversary they had a surprise: Jane was pregnant. They became the biological parents of Elizabeth. All three of these children grew up to be very good looking people. I met all three of them when I went to visit Jane in Hereford, Pembrokeshire. Jane was a widow then; Ken had died fairly young.

Ken loved to play jokes on people especially his friends. There was the day one friend got back at him. In his study Ken's phone rang. "This is the Bishop of Plymouth here", said a deep voice. In those days we still addressed a Bishop as my lord so Ken replied, "Good morning my lord", then answering the questions being asked Ken replied "Yes my lord" "no my Lord" then at the other end of the phone came a bellow of laughter. Knowing he had been fooled he shouted down the phone "you silly fool".

About an hour later the phone rang in Ken's study, he picked up the phone to hear, "This is the Bishop of Plymouth here". Ken replied, "Oh shut up you silly fool". Oh dear, this time it really was the bishop! Poor Ken, he naturally felt terrible and apologised. I don't remember if he explained to the Bishop, but I do remember one Sunday when we had a Confirmation service and the Bishop came to Ken's house for tea before the service. Now Jane was a Psychologist and I remember (I was also there for tea) the Bishop, with a twinkle in his eye, said to Jane, "Jane if one of your clients came to you to tell you they had made a mistake by calling his Bishop a silly fool, how would you help him?"

Ken did not become a Vicar. He went back into the RAF but this time as a chaplain. The family had to move around a lot as Ken was stationed in several places. I remember at one point the family had to move the

Island of Gan. I still have a cowrie shell with a church and my name carved into it, which they gave me.

The next Curate after Ken was John Young (father of my second Goddaughter). John had been a teacher before he was ordained. When John had done his three year curacy he became the head of Religious Education at Northgate School in Ipswich, then Chaplain and senior lecturer at Bishop Otter College in Chichester. I visited them there a few times. His next move was to become Chaplain and senior lecturer at St. John's College York and Curate at St. Paul's York. He then became Diocesan Evangelist, then Canon and Prebendary of York Minster. Some people know John from the York Courses which he began. He wrote a very helpful book with the title "The Case against Christ"; this has of recent years been revised. John is now retired and lives in York.

When John left St. Jude's Robin Toley came as Curate. When he came to the end of his curacy he did not become a Vicar. He went on to do a great work as a Church Pastoral Aid Society traveling Secretary. He also became an honorary Curate at St. John's Harbourne. Robin married Ann who was a member of the congregation. Sadly before Robin left St. Jude's he developed a serious liver complaint. He was not fully well when he went on to other spheres of service. Those of us who knew Robin well were so sad when we heard he had died. He had gone to Australia on some assignment and was taken seriously ill; we found out he had died at the side of the road. He left a widow Ann and two daughters. Ann is a teacher and she bravely carried on and brought up the two girls. They are now married.

Ten very happy years at St. Jude's and I knew the time had come for me to look for another parish. I began the search for the place for the next place I was to serve. Little did I realise that this time it would be as assistant curate.

Chapter 14

1974-1990

Knowing when it is time to leave a parish is never easy. While at St. Jude's my search for the next parish began. This time I did not have the direction I had when I left my Theological College. I scanned the Church newspapers, answered one or two adverts where they were looking for a woman colleague in the London area. I wanted to be where God wanted me to be. Trying to discern God's will seemed to get harder. Positions that appealed to me turned out not to be the right place. There were two parishes in Devon. They were not of my evangelical persuasion. As others had done before me I wondered: should I consider this. One parish had a part time chaplaincy at a nearby hospital. Having done a short assistant chaplaincy at the Royal Devon and Exeter Hospital, I was quite drawn to that. It turned out not to be the right place. The second parish, still in Devon and quite near to Exeter, needed a colleague who would be willing to visit in the prison situated on the edge of the parish. Apart from visiting two prisons as part of my training at college, I was not sure about this. It seemed to me I would need some further training to enter into this type of ministry. It was a relief when the incumbent said he did not think I was suitable.

I was feeling a bit low and wondering what was going to happen when I received a communication from the Church Pastoral Aid Society; a large parish in Braintree in Essex was seeking a woman colleague. I contacted the Vicar over the phone. We arranged that I should travel on the overnight train from Plymouth. I was to stay for the week-end, which would give plenty of time to discuss the details of the position and to see the Parish. After arriving at Paddington I then had to get a train to Braintree. The Vicarage was only a short walk from the station. As I walked along the road I observed how dirty and run down the area looked. I hasten to add it is totally different now. The whole area has been renovated over the years. Braintree in 1974 was a fast developing town.

The Reverend Richard Mulrenan was the vicar. He was an older man; he and his wife Grace had been missionaries in China for many years. I was a little in awe of him to begin with. Dick (I was not able to call him Dick until he retired!) and his wife Grace had to leave China towards the end of the Second World War. It was not safe for them to remain any longer. When I arrived at the vicarage I was warmly greeted by Dick and Grace plus their very large yellow Labrador Bruce. Bruce put me at ease straight away. He showed he approved of me no matter what his owners might have thought!

Braintree is a market town. St. Michael's Church is next to the town centre. The Vicarage was across a small road opposite the church. To begin with I had agreed to occupy a flat within the Vicarage which was quite large. However, the Diocese had decided to sell the Vicarage and buy a modern house about a quarter of a mile from the town centre. Things were changing; it was now considered necessary for the vicar's study to be near the front door, and toilet facilities next to it. The new house had been built like that so it was ideal. The idea was that the family was not disturbed by all the comings and goings that take place in a vicarage. St. Michael's had a curate's house and this became my home for the time I was there.

Dick was a man of vision as well as being a good business man. Under his direction the old vicarage was bought from the Diocese. The house was renovated; the two largest rooms on the ground floor were made into one and became a small church hall. Being a large house, all the rooms on the top floor became teaching rooms for all the various groups in the church. Before Dick retired a new large church hall was built alongside the house, still leaving a large part of the garden intact. The old church hall in the small road leading into the town was demolished; the land was sold for redevelopment. This area became an arcade of small shops. The money from the sale paid towards the renovation of the old vicarage into a very good church centre plus the building of the larger Church hall. There was now room for all the activities that took place.

At this time St. Michael's had a daughter church, St. Paul's. The Reverend John Casselton was the Curate in charge. When I joined the staff I was so pleased to find John was a member of the team. I knew John quite well from my years at St. Jude's. At that time he had been the curate at St. Mary's Upton in Torquay.

St. Michael's was a large parish; there were 6,000 houses and a population of around 16,000 people.

My weekend interview was very busy and quite tiring. As Dick drove me round the parish I soon realised how much bigger it was than St. Jude's. It was a great deal more spread out. Dick pointed out to me that I would need a car to get around. He also outlined what my ministry would be; he made it clear that my position would be different from my time at Plymouth. "If we agree that this is the right place for you,

My last day at St. Michael's, Braintree

1987 Ordination as Deacon at Saffron Walden

you will be the assistant curate", he told me. "You will be expected to take an equal share in leading the services and preaching." Although I would be able to take part in leading the communion services and administer the bread and the wine, I could not conduct the communion service as a whole. "I will require you to prepare the young people for confirmation", Dick informed me. I did prepare the young people for all of the sixteen years I spent at St. Michael's and thoroughly enjoyed this part of my ministry. After three months of preparation I found we had a warm bond of fellowship together. All these years later I still receive letters from two people. One who was divorced from his first wife wrote and shared his sorrow with me. Then after several years he wrote and told me of his second marriage and how happy he and his second wife were together. They write each year to tell me what they have been doing through the year, and what they are doing in their local church. The other person is a nurse who is now middle aged; now many years after her divorce she has remarried and settled down happily. What a privilege it has been to share the experiences of these two people.

Once I was ordained as a Deaconess my ministry expanded; I could now conduct funerals and baptise. We had many baptisms. When baptism was requested the parents of babies and small children were given preparation before the baptism took place. This involved meeting the parents in their homes and explaining to them what baptism really meant, their responsibility and that of the godparents, if they were going to have them.

When Dick retired I had the responsibility for everyone who made enquiries about baptism. An unmarried middle-aged lady came requesting baptism and confirmation. I prepared her for both. I was really nervous about baptising her. The time came (it took place during the evening service), I found it quite emotional. I think it reminded me of my own adult baptism. She was confirmed at another church as she had missed the service at St. Michael's which had taken place earlier in the year. I was able to go with her and act as her sponsor. She wrote me a lovely letter thanking me for my preparation. She had a good sense of humour, she wrote, "I must be the biggest baby you have ever baptised"!

It was during the interregnum I prepared several adults for confirmation. As the day for the confirmation drew near one lady, who was a rather a nervous soul, confided to me she felt she would not be able to get up off her knees after the bishop had confirmed her. I took great care showing her how she could get up without falling over. The inevitable happened, as she tried to get up off her knees she fell forward into the bishop's lap!!! He just kindly took her hands and helped her to her feet. Maybe it is just as well people stand these days!

Another area of my ministry at St. Michael's was to lead the monthly local meeting of the "Ladies Home Mission Union"; this name was eventually changed to "Women's Action". Some people were not happy with the change of name, "It sounds militant", they said. The "Ladies Home Mission Union" was part of the work of the Church Pastoral Aid Society. St. Michael's was a Church Pastoral Aid Society church. Part of my stipend came from the C.P.A.S.

When Dick and Grace retired, Grace was not able to find anyone to take over the leadership of the Women's Fellowship, which meant I now had the leadership of two meetings as well as my other work. Fortunately, one of the younger women did take over the leadership of the Young Wives' Group, and a member of The Mothers' Union took over the leadership of their meeting. I was very grateful.

The first few years of my time at St. Michael's, the curate of the daughter church and I became joint chaplains of the small local hospital in the town. St. Michael's has a Church of England primary school. When the town was renovated the school moved into a new building a short distance from the town. It was a good modern building with its own grounds and playing fields. Everyone was so pleased that the school kept its family atmosphere. Both teachers and parents were fearful this might be lost. One of our church wardens, Gordon Cornell, was the head teacher. The deputy head plus a few of the teachers were members of the congregation.

A short while after I began my ministry at St. Michael's I was invited by the Gordon Cornell to give religious instruction to one of the top classes once a week. The Vicar took the other top class; he also led the morning assembly once a week. On the whole the children were well behaved. There were only a few occasions when I had to send a child to the head teacher, because it had persisted in being disruptive.

Now and again I went to speak at the morning assembly. I still remember when the theme for the day was "obedience to God's Laws". Gordon had given me permission to take my Labrador Bob into school; Sam had died by this time. I wanted to use him as a visual aid of obedience. He was an obedient dog after being trained, but I did wonder if, with all the excitement, he would let me down. Fortunately for me each time I gave him a command he obeyed immediately. It really got the point over, or should I say Bob got the point over! Needless to say he was a hit with the children who were allowed to pet him when the assembly was finished.

The Young People

The children and young people of St. Michael's belonged to the Covenanter Organisation. These were the days when children were beginning to dislike the idea of "Sunday School". The young people from twelve years upwards were known as senior Covenanters, the seven to eleven years old were Jucos (Junior Covenanters). Only the four years old to six years old were called Sunday school. As time went on this age group was also incorporated into the movement. If I remember rightly they became Climbers.

We had a very good youth group. We were fortunate in having dedicated leaders. I spent a short time leading the girl covenanter group. When a leader became available I was able to hand over and concentrate on my other commitments. My main contact with the teenagers was when they made the request to be confirmed. (As mentioned earlier this was an area of my ministry.)

One Sunday during the evening service I was leading the prayers. After his sermon Dick gave out the wrong number for the next hymn, while the congregation took the correct number of the hymn from the hymn board. It just so happened that the words of both hymns went to the same tune; thus Dick was heartily singing the words of the hymn number he had given out and the congregation were singing the words of the correct hymn. Dick loved singing and was completely oblivious to the fact that the congregation were singing different words. Our young people (who all sat together in the first three pews) were really struggling to keep their amusement under control. As I was leading the prayers I thought I would help them to control themselves, so I began, "We will begin our prayers tonight with a time of silence". This was quite the wrong thing to do, several of the youngsters had got the giggles by this time and quite a few of them were stuffing their handkerchiefs into their mouths to get their giggles under control. After the service I had to explain to Dick about the young people's mirth. He had no idea of what was going on or why. I think he eventually understood.

A serious situation

I had not been at St. Michael's very long when Dick phoned me to say he needed to speak to me about something that had occurred concerning me. It was so serious he was considering asking me to leave the parish. He made an appointment and came to my home to speak to me. I found out that someone from St. Paul's (the daughter church) had taken a strong dislike to me. It appeared they had gone to Dick and accused me of saying something about Dick which was not only untrue but also of a sexual nature. When Dick arrived he came to the point immediately (he was quite an austere man), "If this is true", he said, "I will have to ask you to go". I was shocked and told him I had said nothing of the sort. My mind raced trying to think if I had said anything that could have been misconstrued. I could think of nothing. Not knowing who the person was didn't help. Who had I been having a conversation with at St. Paul's? I just could not think. As we talked I became aware that Dick was not at all sure I was not guilty. I was quite distressed and ended up in tears. Dick prayed with me and left. I did not sleep that night. My mind went over and over all that Dick had said to me. What had I said to the person who had gone to Dick to cause them to make this accusation? Why did they dislike me? I found myself becoming really angry at whoever had done this; I was also sad that Dick had believed this of me. Then I became aware that I could not honestly lead the services on Sunday or take part in a communion service feeling as I did. Since I had come to know Christ as my Saviour, and learning from the scriptures that if there is anything between a Christian brother or sister one must go and put it right, especially so if one is taking communion. Matthew, chapter five, verse twenty four: "therefore, if you are offering your gift at the altar and there remember that your brother has something against you, leave your gift there in front of the altar. First go and be reconciled to your brother; then come and offer your gift". These are the words of Jesus. Although they do not apply to the Holy Communion we celebrate, the principle applies.

Warren Wiersbe in his commentary on Matthew writes, "We must go to our brother and must do it quickly". "It has been well said, that the person who refuses to forgive his brother destroys the very bridge on which he himself must walk".

The next morning (Saturday), in a distressed state, I cycled down the hill from where I lived to see Dick and tell him how I felt. I rang the vicarage bell and Dick came to the door; he asked me in and led me to the kitchen where he and Grace were having breakfast. Feeling rather sick I began to say why I had come; Dick interrupted telling me he and Grace were discussing the situation. I was then able to tell them how angry and upset I was. I don't know if Grace had managed to help Dick to see I was not guilty, but Dick had come to realise I had nothing to do with what had been said about me. They had come to the conclusion that for whatever reason it was a malicious attack on me. At this point all three of us were in tears. We prayed with one another, and I went home comforted. When I got home I confessed to the Lord how angry I had been and asked Him to take away my anger and give me the grace to forgive the person who was responsible for the whole situation. Whoever it was, He knew, I did not.

Sunday came. I was able to worship and lead the services as my peace of heart was restored. It was through this that my Heavenly Father showed me something about myself. My hurt and anger stemmed from my childhood, when so many times I was accused of doing something I had not done, and not being believed when I tried to explain. Over the years there have been occasions when I have had to fight this personal battle again. How weak our trust is and how difficult we find it is to hand our problems over to our Lord and leave them there!

St. Michael's was known as a training parish. Students came to us on placement. The men stayed at the vicarage, the women stayed with me at the Curate's house. Apart from attending all the services plus all the various weekly meetings, the students spent time each week with us learning more about ministry in a parish. They were given opportunity to lead some of the meetings as well as to lead a service on Sunday and to preach. It was part of our brief to give them constructive criticism. At the end of their placement we had to fill out a report on their progress and send it to their college. One of the instructions I had was to take the student visiting and let them observe a difficult situation. I took my student to visit a lady who had a rather difficult medical condition. She insisted that every person who visited must see her operation scars!! Apart from a couple of friends I was the only other person to visit her. I walked with the student to the lady's home. Once inside and having introduced the student, this dear soul said to me; "Oh Miss Lawrence, I must show you my new medical bra and corset". She then opened a sideboard drawer took out these rather large garments and spread them out for our inspection. Making what I thought were the appropriate remarks at the same time observing any reaction from the student, it was very hard to keep a straight face. When we left the house and were out of sight my student was convulsed with laughter. When she could she said, "I just don't know how I managed to keep a straight face through all that". Needless to say she passed the test.

CHAPTER 15

Ordination

1974-1990

After much debate women were at last to be ordained as Deacons. Together with nine other women I was ordained Deacon on Saturday June 13th 1987. The service was conducted by the then Bishop of Chelmsford the Right Reverend John Waine at St. Mary's Church Saffron Walden.

One of the Deaconesses of whom we were very fond was ordained after sixty years of service as a Deaconess. She was the longest serving Deaconess in the Diocese!

There were thirty three Deaconesses ordained in three separate services across the Chelmsford Diocese; it was a very happy day for me. Bernard (Barney) my Vicar and Rosemary his wife put on a celebratory lunch at the Vicarage.

The following Tuesday at our weekly staff meeting Barney announced, "Now you are an ordained Deacon Helen, you can conduct weddings; next Saturday there are four, so over to you". Barney had already checked out if the couples were happy about a woman conducting their services, they were quite happy. A report of the first wedding that day found its way into the local paper, with a photograph of me with the couple. The headline read "DEACON MAKES HISTORY". "Fame at last" I quipped.

Was I nervous? Yes, I was. Yet, at the same time I felt it was a privilege to be able to do this. St. Michael's church had quite a lot of weddings so I conducted several; I was able to prepare the couples as well. Barney had, of course, prepared the first four couples before he asked me to conduct their wedding services.

Church Family Holidays

Apart from the everyday affairs of parish life there are other areas of ministry that stand out in my memory. Who thought of it originally I cannot remember, but someone came up with the idea of having Church Family Holidays, and not just the Parish Church. All the ministers and church leaders of the main denominations in Braintree got together to explore the idea and to plan how this could be organised.

These holidays took place for some years, families and single people spending a week together. It was a good time; we got to know each other better as well as having good fun and fellowship.

Each year we rented a school (a different area each year); among other places we went to Exeter, Harrowgate, Sherbourne in Somerset, and Devon. The schools were ideal as they had large grounds and nearly all of them had their own swimming pool, plus a sports hall: ideal for outdoor or indoor activities.

Families were free to remain together or join with other families to go out for the day. Some days two or three families would join up and include single people, especially if they did not have their own transport, and go off to visit some area of interest or any place they would like to go. Others stayed in the school and grounds to play tennis or games, while others relaxed in the grounds or the school if the weather was not so good.

Some of the ministers and leaders visited the school beforehand to see what facilities it offered. Then we were able to allocate rooms accordingly. We realised teenagers did not want to be with their parents all the time but to be with friends, so we arranged dormitories for the boys and for the girls if they wanted to be with their friends.

The catering staff at some of the schools remained and catered for us, which was very good. When a school did not have this arrangement we did our own catering. It was early days and not every school had washing up machines, so we made up rotas for teams of people to wash and dry up, and to clear away and lay the tables for the meal. This proved to be a good time for sharing and getting to know each other. This was not something we planned to happen yet it turned out to be a good time of fellowship around the chores.

At the end of a busy day enjoying ourselves we came together in the evening for a time of worship and reflection led by the ministers and leaders.

Those of us who were ministers made ourselves available to help or guide anyone who had a problem and wanted to discuss it. Over the years we did have to handle one or two difficult situations.

A lot of people were blessed through these holidays.

Bad Dog—Good Dog

As there was only one or two of us, we were able to take our dogs with us. My first dog, a Labrador Retriever cross really blotted his copybook and mine. Sam decided he wanted a swim (I did not have my eyes on him at that moment) and he dived into the swimming pool. This incurred the wrath of a school official who happened to be around that day. After that Sam had to remain on his lead in the school grounds. Any further swims had to be when we visited the seaside!

Another time Sam became a sort of a hero. The year this happened we were at St. Ethelburga's School near Harrogate in Yorkshire. It was a day when two or three families visited a lovely area at Knaresborough; together with Sam I was invited to go with them. We had just finished our picnic lunch at the side of the river, when we heard someone screaming. Two teenage girls (not connected with us) were in a boat in the middle of the river; they had lost an oar, the boat was drifting towards a weir and the girls were now panicking. "Sam, come here", I called to Sam who was nearby. "Good boy, go fetch", I commanded pointing to where the oar was also drifting. Sam in his usual way dived into river and began to swim towards the oar. I kept on encouraging him, "Good boy, fetch the stick". At the same time I was frightened at what I had asked Sam to do. The river was wide and deep. I expected Sam to grab the oar and swim to the opposite side of the river, where hopefully someone would get the oar and get it out of the river. Sam astonished us all as he grabbed the handle of the oar and swam in a sort of half circle back to our side of the river. Some of the teenage boys in our party dragged Sam out of the water; they then ran with the oar to a line of boats moored nearby. They hopped from one boat to the other and got the oar back to the girls whose boat had by now drifted to the side of the river near to the moored boats. That day Sam was the hero of the day! A loud cheer went up from both sides of the river, as people observed what had happened. I will never forget the gentleman who approached me and in a broad Yorkshire accent said, "Eee by gum lass that is some dog to have". We all reckoned if a local newspaper reporter had been around Sam would have been front page news! Needless to say, Sam got lots of fuss that day and far too many treats than were good for him!!

Home Made Entertainment

At the end of each holiday, the evening before we went home we had "Home Produced Entertainment". We discovered a great deal of talent among the folk from all the churches. The talent we discovered among the St. Michael's families was put to use for entertainment at Harvest Suppers and other church events. Although asked several times I was very reluctant to take part in this. After a few years they eventually persuaded me. So, before the next holiday and after a lot of thought I made the decision to be Eliza Doolittle singing the song "All I want is a room somewhere" from the show "My Fair Lady" and, of course, in a cockney accent!

One of our young people from St. Michael's was training as a beautician, she made up my face, I borrowed a professional wig from my hairdresser, wore a long dress and carried a basket of flowers. Another member of St. Michael's helped me by accompanying me on the piano. We rehearsed several times before the event. I was amazed when I looked in the mirror; I did not look like me at all! Later in the year after the next church holiday, at one of the Harvest Suppers, I was asked to do this again. So with our young beautician making up my face, my wearing the long dress carrying the basket of flowers, I sang again with the same cockney accent. At the Harvest Supper when it came to my contribution, Gordon Cornell (our church warden) who was acting as MC announced me as an artist they had got from London at great expense. In the audience sat Barney the Vicar with one of our parishioners next to him who had not been to any of the church holidays. "Who is that?" said Jack. "You know who it is", said Barney. "No, I have no idea", replied Jack. "It's our Helen", said Barney. "Well, I would never have guessed, I can hardly believe it", said Jack. It took a long time for me to live it down.

Times of Mission

During the years I was at Braintree the Evangelist Billy Graham was in England holding evangelistic campaigns. One year the meetings were televised to a local cinema or church hall. Together with others I was asked to become an adviser at the meetings to those who made an indication that they wanted to make a commitment to Christ.

Then in 1984 Billy Graham came to Ipswich. The meetings were held in the Portman Road Football Stadium. Again with other people I was asked to become an adviser; we attended preparation meetings for this. We were to go down from the stands to the front of the podium together with the people who went forward as a response to what they heard as Billy Graham talked. We advisers were directed to people who expressed a wish to make a commitment or a recommitment to faith in Jesus Christ. It was a wonderful time of seeing God at work in people's lives, and a privilege to be part of it. As advisers it was part of our job to see that people who responded were directed to their own church or, if they were not already members, they would be directed to a church where they would get spiritual support.

Two years after this event the Parochial Church Council at St. Michael's felt the time was right for us as a church to have our own church mission.

Ian Knox a missioner from up north was invited to come and speak to the PCC and discuss with us what would be expected of us all. I remember his words to us at that meeting, "I am the missioner but you are the ones who will do the work". We certainly did do the work, before and after the mission! Our first task was to deliver letters from the Vicar and the PCC to the people's homes, explaining who we were and that we would be visiting them very soon. In those days St. Michael's had a daughter church, St. Paul's. Some years after the mission St. Paul's became a Parish in its own right. Braintree town was rapidly expanding as were the areas around the town.

Following the delivery of the letters to all six thousand homes in the parish, members of the congregations of both St. Michael's and St. Paul's went out in twos and visited each home in the parish.

We also set up a Prayer Triplets scheme. Groups of three people met in homes each week all over the parish to pray for the mission. When any special needs arose these were telephoned to the groups (not many folk had computers then) and they prayed accordingly. As we visited we were invited into many homes. We had many useful conversations, however, we realised not everyone was going to respond positively. We discovered a lot of goodwill was built up as a result of our visiting.

It was an amazing ten days. It was not only at the Sunday services that Ian Knox preached, the events through the week, as well as the organisations that took place, were all part of the mission. Invitations went out inviting people in the parish to come. It was a very busy time, there was something going on each day. Each day began with a time of prayer.

I will never forget the last Sunday of the mission. At the end of each service (we had four in the day, 8 am, 9.30 am, 11am, and 6.30 pm) Ian Knox asked that if there was anyone who had made a commitment to Christ during the last ten days including this Sunday, would they come to the front of the church he would like to pray for them. He had also planned for leaders in the church family to stand at various points in the church and act as counsellors to people who had made a commitment. I became one of the counsellors. Our brief was to help the people who came forward to understand exactly what they had committed themselves to and then pray with them. Each of us had undergone instruction to enable us to take on this task.

It was a remarkable time and emotional. As Ian gave out the invitation people came forward, families came forward hand in hand with each other, people on their own, all ages. Bernard and I stood each side of the church with tears running down our face, tears of joy, tears of relief that the church as a whole had been obedient to what we believed God had asked us to do, and tears of praise for what God had done over these past ten days.

When the mission was over, together with the PCC, we set up nurture groups for people to be nurtured in their new found faith.

How God Spoke in an Awesome Way

It was during the weeks and months we spent in preparation for the mission that I had what I can only call an awesome experience. One afternoon I was preparing to lead a prayer meeting in the evening (Bernard, the Vicar, had gone down with the flu and in his place I was to lead the monthly meeting of all the prayer triplet groups). As I prayed in my study I had a vision: it began with a picture of one person in a single prison cell, the picture then changed to two or three people in a single prison cell, and again it changed to a larger group of people in a large prison cell. I did not know what it all meant, but somehow I was convinced this was something I had to share with the people who would be at the prayer meeting in the evening. I was also convinced I must tell Bernard about this first so I phoned Rosie (Bernard's wife) who said it was alright for me to go and see Bernard. When I told Bernard he too was convinced I should share this vision with the people at the prayer meeting. I arrived at the small church hall, with shaking knees and a thumping heart I shared the vision with them. As soon as I finished one of our readers said, "Helen, God is convicting me through this. I am so scared of having to speak to someone straight out about Jesus. I am one of those people in the prison cell". After that several people admitted they too felt they were in a prison cell being held back with fear of speaking openly about their faith; then I had to admit that it affected me as well. I feared the mission itself, the responsibility of what we had taken on. Where was my faith? Everyone agreed that night that if we did not repent of our attitude, the mission when it took place would not be blessed. We all realised God had spoken to us at St. Michael's as a whole. The prayer meeting was a very blessed time that night.

I think you will agree from what I have already imparted to you about the mission that God did truly bless St. Michael's church. As I look back I remind myself what a privilege it was to be involved during that time.

Health Problems and Retirement

For some years I had suffered from severe migraine headaches. My doctor explained I was suffering from what he termed as "classical migraine". Basically, every time I relaxed, say on my day off, I went down with one of these episodes. Several times I would be on the point of going on holiday. I would pack up the car, drive off. Go a few miles and bang, I would just have to turn round go home and to bed. Being determined I did not want to give in to it, which did not help. It got me in the end. Then other health issues began to appear. I had hoped I would retire at sixty five, as I approached sixty it became evident I would have to retire early. I had spent sixteen years at St. Michael's as assistant curate. Bernard and friends in the parish helped me make the decision. Now here I was again placing the situation into God's hands. It was a hard decision to make; it threw up several questions. I did not have a home to go to, where would I live? There were a few people who were keen for me to stay in the parish or nearby. When I retired it was understood that one did not live in the parish once you were no longer part of the ministry team. I understood this and had no intention of doing so.

In one way it was quite exciting looking for the right area to live and a home to live in. God is faithful and I eventually found a home in Kirby Cross next to Frinton on Sea in Essex thirty four miles away from Braintree; as it happens I used to make the journey there every couple of months to visit a few of our parishioners who were in care homes there. A retired priest I knew well told me he had some friends who wanted to sell their bungalow. They had to move for health reasons. The people who lived next door but one to them were very keen to buy their bungalow. However, they had to sell their own bungalow to be able to buy the other one. It was ideal in every way and fulfilled all the requirements of the Church of England Pensions Board to purchase it for me to rent from them. It had a fairly large garden which was ideal as my four year old yellow Labrador dog was going to move with me.

I was sad to go but at the same time I did have a sense of excitement at what God had in store for me in the future.

CHAPTER 16

Retirement

1990—

What I would do when I retired is something I thought about a lot. The idea of sitting around doing little or nothing is just not me. While still working I thought one of the things that appealed to me would be to learn to draw and paint. I remember that at school I was never able to draw much at all, it was always a struggle to get things down correctly.

When I required a visual aid of any kind to use for a family service, I always had to get someone to draw it for me. My limit was pin men! I mostly relied on objects to illustrate the point I was getting over. This took a lot of time and energy.

I thought back to when I was child, how when I wandered in the fields near where we were living at the time, I would observe the sky, the patterns the clouds would make, the different kinds of trees, and different shades of colour; then, when I was able to go on holiday years later, in the British Isles and abroad, as well as the time I lived in South Africa, the beautiful surroundings. I loved the mountains, the way they changed colour through the day. I loved the beauty of creation and longed to be able to put down on paper what I could see.

After recovering from the exhaustion of moving and all it entailed, and settling down in my new home, I made enquiries about classes. I discovered there were classes for beginners on how to draw and paint. The first classes I attended were only a mile away at Walton-on-the-Naze. I had a car so it was easy for me to get there. It was a great time of learning for me. I soon discovered, as with other things in life, art is something one never stops learning about. Over the years painting has become a source of joy. It is not only absorbing but therapeutic.

Together with a woman clergy friend I went on a few painting week-ends to different parts of the country, the most memorable was to a farm in Devon. The farmer's wife was the tutor. Each day she gave us instruction, after which we returned to the house to a superb lunch. The farmer's wife was a great cook. Each day she took us out to different parts of Dartmoor. Wow! What a challenge: to be able to get down on paper a sky that was changing by the minute. It meant we had to memorise the skyscape as we saw it and paint it. The scenery was stunning; it was all so invigorating as well as the challenge to paint what we saw.

My friend Pat and I became members of the Society for Amateur Artists; it is now known as The Society for All Artists. Through this society I have received great encouragement and still do through its magazines.

After attending several classes, some with professional artists, I came across a painting workshop. This was a group of people of varying ages; we met together at a community hail very near to Frinton. One of the joys of this group was that we could all help one another. Each of us was at a different stage; we had all learned different techniques which we could share with each other; we had also learned ways of correcting mistakes we had made. We were able to share these with each other. We were all amateur artists. This group still meets. Twice a year at the Community Hall we put on an exhibition and sale of our work. Over the years I belonged to this group, and to my surprise and pleasure, I sold some of my paintings.

I now live in Cambridge. I have joined a U3A (University of the Third Age) painting class. The class I was able to join meets in the autumn and winter term. This is good because belonging to a group like this one is committed to going each week. Being on one's own there always seems to be something more important to do.

Relaxation and Ministry

Frinton is a good place for walking. My Labrador Bob and I walked for miles when I first retired, especially in the winter. I would drive to the village of Great Holland and park outside the church, then Bob and I would walk through the farm, around the edge of the fields, across the golf course, then along the sea wall, and if the tide was out we went along the beach until we came to a reserve at the beginning of Holland on Sea. Other days we began in Frinton and walked the sea wall or the beach until we nearly got to Clacton. Near the area where I was living there were farm fields reached by a public footpath which went along to the nearby village of Kirby le Soken. Here the owners of the farmland had set aside, an area around the edges of the fields not sown with wheat. Dog owners were at liberty to walk their dogs here. Bob's favourite game in this area was to chase the rabbits. He could never catch them of course but he loved to poke his muzzle into the entrance of their warrens. I often wondered if he sent down a message: "I'll get you next time". When the wheat was harvested and put into large bales in the field I used to play hide and seek with Bob; I hid until he found me.

I became a member of St. Mary's Church in Frinton. After I had been there awhile the Vicar, the Revd. Robin Elphick, came to see me and asked, "Would I consider taking some part in the ministry?" There were a few care homes in the area. I began to visit in these homes. There were elderly members of St. Mary's church resident there. I also visited elderly and housebound members of the church. Then I helped at a few of the services, and was able to take some of the funerals as well. I enjoyed the opportunity to have a small part in the ministry of St. Mary's.

Ordination

Meanwhile the debate about women being ordained as priests went on. In 1993 retired women like myself in the Chelmsford Diocese were contacted by the Suffragen Bishop of Colchester to ask us if we would consider being ordained priest. Being retired I did not think it would apply to me, neither did a fellow retired deacon (Pat Cotton); she had also retired to Frinton. Pat and I were not only surprised but extremely pleased. Because Pat and I had been in the ministry a long time we realised that, together with other women of our age, we were pioneers of women in the ministry in the Church of England. We had been Lady (Parish) workers, Deaconesses, seven years as Deacons, and now we were about to be ordained priests. "Halleluiah!"

Women from the Archdeaconry of Colchester
about to be ordained as Priest

Robin Elphick   Me   Bishop of Chelmsford

30th April. Day of Ordination to Priesthood.

There were quite a few preliminaries to go through, a few interviews as well as one with one of the bishops. My interview was with the Suffragan Bishop of Colchester, The Right Revd. Michael Vickers. I was happy about that; I knew him quite well, so I felt quite relaxed. The interview was to ascertain whether I had a calling to the priesthood. As far as I was concerned this was the culmination of my original call when I was in South Africa! There was a short period of preparation for all the women, those who were retired as well as those who were already working as deacons.

Before we were ordained as priests we had to show that we were engaged in ministry in the parish. As well as what I was already doing, there had to be a specific area of ministry in which I was engaged. I officially became chaplain to the Home for the Blind. There was a large care home as well to which I became chaplain (sadly because of the economic climate this home had to close). I was chaplain there for a short while after I was priested. I remained chaplain to the Home for the Blind, visiting regularly, taking communion services and, where requested by the family, I conducted the funeral of those who had died.

Before we women were priested we had a certain amount of preparation. A few days before the ordination we went into retreat. The day before the ordination we attended a "Quiet Day"; this was conducted by the Bishop of Chelmsford, The Right Reverend John Waine.

The day ended with the Bishop's ordination charge to us all. We returned to the Retreat House at Pleshy, just near Chelmsford, Then came the great day!

On the thirtieth of April 1994 fifty three women in the Diocese of Chelmsford were ordained as priests.

Chelmsford Cathedral is not large. To accommodate all the families and friends, as well as the clergy, necessitated three services through the day. There was one in the morning, one in the afternoon, and one in the evening. Those of us who were being ordained in the afternoon service remained at the retreat house, likewise those in the evening service. I was in the evening group. There was such an air of rejoicing; it was difficult for those of us awaiting our turn to remain quiet and prayerful. The last group of us moved off in our cars and made our way into Chelmsford and the Cathedral. Parking had been made available for us in the Diocesan House garden. As I walked through the garden to the Cathedral I managed to see one or two of my friends and greet them. It was so good to see them there.

Before the service and once we had robed we stood before the Commissary (the Bishops lawful representative) who read the Preface to us and the Declaration of Assent. We then affirmed our belief, and took our oath of Allegiance and our oath of Canonical Obedience. (See below)

ORDINATION by the Right Reverend **JOHN by Divine Permission BISHOP OF CHELMSFORD** in the Cathedral Church of Chelmsford on the **30th** day of **April 1994**

DECLARATION made and Oaths taken and subscribed in the presence of the Bishop on the 30th day of April 1994 by the undersigned persons about to be admitted to the Holy Order of Priest

DECLARATION OF ASSENT

PREFACE (Spoken by the Bishop or Commissary)

The Church of England is part of the One, Holy, Catholic and Apostolic Church worshipping the one true God, Father, Son and Holy Spirit. It professes the faith uniquely revealed in the Holy Scriptures and set forth in the catholic creeds, which faith the Church is called upon to proclaim afresh in each generation. Led by the Holy Spirit, it has borne witness to Christian truth in its historic formularies, the Thirty-nine Articles of Religion, the Book of Common Prayer and the Ordering of Bishops, Priests and Deacons. In the declaration you are about to make will you affirm your loyalty to this inheritance of faith as your inspiration and guidance under God in bringing the grace and truth of Christ to this generation and making him known to those in your care?

I Helen Lawrence do so affirm, and accordingly declare my belief in the faith which is revealed in the Holy Scriptures and set forth in the catholic creeds and to which the historic formularies of the Church of England bear witness; and in public prayer and administration of the sacraments, I will use only the forms of service which are authorised or allowed by Canon.

OATH OF ALLEGIANCE

I Helen Lawrence do swear that I will be faithful and bear true allegiance to Her Majesty Queen Elizabeth II, her heirs and successors, according to law: So help me God.

OATH OF CANONICAL OBEDIENCE

I Helen Lawrence do swear by Almighty God that I will pay true and canonical obedience to the Lord Bishop of Chelmsford and his successors, in all things lawful and honest: So help me God.

DATED this 30th day of April One thousand nine hundred and ninety-four.

We were able to invite three clergy whom we knew to lay hands on us at the moment of ordination. I chose the Revd. Robin Elohick who was the Rector of St. Mary's Frinton at the time; his wife Jane was able to come to the service, as was Mary, David Lumb's wife (David was a former vicar of St. Jude's Plymouth during my time there). I had chosen David as one of the clergy to lay hands on me. David with his wife Mary travelled from Redditch in Worcestershire. They were able to stay with me for a couple of days after the service. The third person was the Revd. Paul Harwood Jones. Paul had been the vicar of Finchingfield, not far from Braintree. I knew Paul and his wife Jacqui very well; he was a dear, valued friend. Jacqui was able to come to the service.

We were restricted to the number of family and friends we could invite. I had thirty five people come to witness the ordination and rejoice with me. What an amazing day!

Those who organised the day were marvellous. Each service was the same. I had wondered if by the evening the bishops and the officiating clergy would be so tired the service would be low key. Not so, it was magnificent. The service was so meaningful, yet, in a sense triumphant. It was also very emotional; I found myself at several points in the service holding on to my emotions.

When the service was over we were invited, if we wished to do so, to have our hands anointed. This was something very significant to me, as it spoke of my future ministry.

From the moment the service was over the cathedral bells rang out across Chelmsford. It must have been about an hour and a half before we left to travel home and the bells were still ringing!

I drove home from Chelmsford on the A12 followed by David and Mary Lumb. I tried to drive carefully knowing I was so exultant as well as tired! I was grateful to arrive home in Kirby Cross in one piece!

David, Mary and I had a light supper together and retired to bed. I imagined I would not sleep too well that night; yet, I did sleep very well. As the three of us attended my church, St. Mary's the next day, there was more rejoicing as friends and parishioners came and greeted me.

I had to come down to earth at some time. I presided at my first communion service just over a week later.

Now I entered into a period of what I would call semi-retirement. In a short while Robin Elphick was moving on to a parish in Norfolk. St. Mary's entered into an interregnum which lasted for seven and half months. Life became quite busy. I was so glad I was not on my own. The Revd. Norman Bedford and his wife Pat retired to Frinton. Norman had been the vicar of St. Mary the Virgin in Dedham in Constable country. I already knew Norman and Pat; I had met them at a retirement conference where I had been asked to speak. Norman was a lovely man and a great colleague to work with. They were also dog lovers so, apart from the ministry, we had something else in common. Norman had to be away from the parish for a couple of weeks. Being the only Anglican clergy person in the parish I found myself called on to take nine funerals in a ten day period. While putting on my robes in the vestry before one of the funerals, I found myself saying to my reflection in the mirror, "I thought I was retired!". During the ten days I visited the homes of the bereaved and conducted the funerals. I visited each of the homes afterwards but not during that ten day period! We did not always have so many funerals in such a short time!

Norman returned and together we carried on the ministry until another Rector was appointed.

In November 1995 the Revd. Andrew Rose was installed as Rector of St. Mary's; he and his wife Pat moved into their new home. Their two children were away at University, Elizabeth (known as Liz) at York and Tim at Luton. Liz is a librarian. After University Tim worked for the Christian organisation EAST to WEST as a trainee evangelist. Those who work for the organisation do a very valuable job among young people who are disadvantaged, working with the young people in schools and supporting them with the issues they have. They have a Police Community Youth Pastor helping those who may be getting into trouble as well as those already on the road to committing crime. After a time Tim felt called into the ministry. He trained, was ordained and is an associate minister at a church in Sunbury.

At Andrew's request Norman and I continued to take part in the ministry at St. Mary's. Everyone at St. Mary's was so sad when Norman became ill. He was ill for a time and then died. I missed him a great deal. Pat, Norman's widow, still lives in Frinton. I see her when I go back to visit.

In 1999 the Revd. Norman Issberner and his wife Marian retired to Frinton. I had known Norman since my days in Braintree. Norman was then the Advisor on Mission and Evangelism in the Diocese of Chelmsford. He retired to Frinton from Clacton-on-Sea where he had been vicar of St. Paul's church from 1993 to 1999, and Rural Dean of St. Osyth from 1994 to 1999.

Andrew invited Norman to join the ministry team. Once again there were two retired clergy to help in the parish. Then in February 2000 the vicar of Christ Church Cockfosters, the Revd. Antony Rees, retired. He together with his wife Margaret carne to live in

Frinton. Once they had settled down Andrew asked Tony to join the team. Now there were three of us. St. Mary's was doing well for clergy! Both Norman and Tony have made a valuable contribution to the ministry at St. Mary's and the surrounding churches. They are both very gifted men and I know their ministry is much valued. Each of us was able to help out at parishes in the Tendring area, as one interregnum was followed by another.

For about two years I helped out at Kirby le Soken with Great Holland. I was frequently at All Saints in Great Holland during their interregnum. I continued helping out there when a new Rector was appointed.

He was not able to be in two places at once. I found the congregation at All Saints would refer to me as their Vicar. I explained several times I could not be their vicar. I really think it was an affectionate way or saying how happy they were that I was with them so often. I came to love them. They were a small congregation, all getting older; the other congregation at St. Michael's Kirby le Soken would have liked them to join them. It was not really in walking distance so they stayed put.

There were some Sundays when we retired clergy found ourselves at two or three churches for the morning service or Holy Communion. There was certainly no thought of us not being needed or wanted.

A Very Happy Occasion

Two years after Andrew's wife Pat died he met a lovely lady called Jenny. She is a licensed Methodist preacher and a trained counsellor. She did not live very far away. Only one or two people knew about this. I had the privilege of being privy to their growing relationship. When it became public knowledge, everyone was so happy for them both. Their wedding was a very joyous occasion. The wedding took place on a day of very warm autumn sunshine. The wedding photographs were taken in the church garden, which was super. There was a funny Incident during Andrew and Jenny's courtship. Andrew had a fairly new Labrador called Beri. From the moment Beri saw Andrew she adored him. One day Andrew had invited Jenny to tea at the Rectory. As they sat together on the sofa Beri got onto the sofa and pushed herself between the two of them; it was as if she was saying, "He is my master not yours". Jenny told me how awful she felt. "I felt like an intruder", she said. Now years later Beri loves both Andrew and Jenny. Andrew and Jenny have now retired to Frinton having spent the last three years of Andrew's paid ministry in Devon.

CHAPTER 17

Remaining Years at Frinton

The time came when I had to slow down. My persistent high blood pressure was causing me problems. Also, I had a respiratory problem. My G.P. treated me for asthma. I certainly had times when I felt I had no air in my lungs, and I had a permanent cough. I was sure this was something more than asthma. I only found out years later that I had Chronic Obstructive Pulmonary Disease. It came to light when Andrew Rose and I were offered a free health check through St. Luke's Hospital for the clergy. I went up to London to have the health check. The Doctor who was doing it saw me again after lot of tests had been carried out. Apart from my raised blood pressure everything was satisfactory, except, as he explained to me, "I am not happy about your chest, I am sending you to the

Middlesex Hospital to see a Cardiac Thoracic Surgeon". After many tests I was told they were writing to my G.P. I did not hear from my doctor and made the assumption I was making more of the situation than was necessary. It was two years later when having a check up with my doctor after a dose of bronchitis, I expressed to him that the bronchitis had made my chest problem worse and it certainly was not asthma. Although irritated with me he took out my file, opened up a few papers, read from them, gave a small gasp and said, "It says here you have Chronic Obstructive Pulmonary Disease and Heart Failure". I was angry, but quickly realised that although those papers had been in my file for two years my doctor had no idea they were in the file. I was not able to find out who had put them there and not informed the doctor. My friends felt this was really not good enough, yet it was too late to do anything about it. Little did I know I was shortly to have my second heart attack.

Before all this happened, in the spring of 1999 my dog Bob's life came to an end. He was fourteen and half years old, a good age for a Labrador. Bob's vet asked me if I was going to have another dog. I said 'no' explaining I did not think it would be fair should I have another heart attack. He suggested I put my name down to look after people's dogs when the owners went on holiday. I did this for ten years.

Although I spent many years trying to find out where my brother Austin was in South Africa, I was never able to track him down. In 1992 I had a communication from May who had been Austin's first wife. They had two daughters Colette and Michelle (known as Miki). Miki was coming to England on holiday. Her mother, May, told her she had an aunt living in England, "When you are there you should try to see her". I had just returned home one day and found a message on the phone to ask me to phone Miki. She was in London. When I phoned her she said she was with a friend who was travelling with her. She would like to come and see me. I gave her instructions on how to get to me. I met them at the station and took them to my home. Over lunch together I said to Miki, "I don't suppose for one moment you know where your father is?" "Yes, I do", she replied, "He lives just eight miles outside Cape Town in Brooklyn". I was amazed. A couple of days later I wrote to Austin explaining I had been trying to find out where he was. We were in touch again.

In October 2003 I flew to South Africa and stayed with Austin and his present wife Phil for three weeks. We spent that time catching up on all the years that had passed. I am so glad I found him, because it was only three years later I flew to South Africa again to conduct his funeral service.

The day before I flew to South Africa the first time I went to see Andrew's wife Pat; she was extremely ill with cancer. She was in hospital in Colchester. I knew I would not see her again. A few days after my arrival at my brother's home, Andrew sent an email to my niece Miki to inform me Pat had died. I was not going to be back in time for her funeral. However, I was able to attend the memorial service for her on my return.

As I settled back into life at home I was sometimes able to take services, sometimes preaching, and helping out at Great Holland though not every week. Austin and I kept in touch by phone frequently; that was good.

The Unexpected Takes Place

Andrew's sister and brother-in-law invited me to their home for a celebration party. It was just before Andrew and I travelled to Hebden Bridge that I discovered from my doctor the results of the tests I had undergone in London. We arrived on Friday evening. Saturday morning quite a few of the guests were watching an important football match. I went off for a walk up the hill next to their home accompanied by three Labrador dogs, Andrew's dog and the family's two Labradors. It was a wonderful June day, very warm and dry. I sat on the hill soaking up the sunshine and the view around. I had been there some time when I decided to come down realising folk might wonder where I was. As I descended the hill my right foot slipped; I did not fall, but came down on my bottom. At that point I my leg twisted, I felt and heard a crack. It was obvious I had done something serious. I was aware I could not call for help no one would have heard me calling from the hill. I tried to encourage the dogs to go home. I could see they thought I was playing a game with them. Feeling a bit desperate I managed to get my sock off my left foot and fastened it as best I could round my right ankle. Holding my injured ankle to keep it from contact with the ground I very slowly slid myself to the base of the hill. Then by hopping (which was agony) I got myself the short distance along the path leading in the garden. I had just got myself seated onto a large breeze block at the edge of the barbecue when Andrew's sister appeared. She had been wondering where I was. I managed to explain I had seriously injured myself, Janet ran to the house to get help. Andrew and his brother-in-law got me to Andrew's car, as they were lifting me into the car I developed angina pains and I had to ask Adrian to get my NGT spray. I had been having angina for a while but it was under some control with medication. Adrian is a medical man (a surgeon) so he understood. Andrew drove me to Calderdale Hospital in Halifax. The doctor in the A & E dept., a Sri Lankan, examined me and confirmed I had seriously broken my ankle. He explained I would have to stay in hospital and would have to undergo an operation. He administered morphine to help with the pain, and explained I would not be able to have a general anaesthetic because my heart was in too poor a condition. Andrew stayed with me for a few hours, then he had to return to Hebden Bridge. The next day after the party he had to return to Frinton.

My ankle was operated on the next day, Sunday. The lady anaesthetist came to explain to me she would administer an epidural and assured me she would be by my side to monitor me during the operation. I was then put into an orthopaedic ward until the eighteenth of June when I was taken by ambulance to Colchester General Hospital. I stayed there until the 25th of June when I was moved to Clacton Town Hospital. It was here I stayed until the 2nd of July when I had my second heart attack and was rushed back to Colchester General Hospital in a blue light ambulance.

I waited in hospital (I had to wait for a bed to become available at the London Chest Hospital). I was eventually moved on the 27th of August. A lot more tests were done and on the 2nd of September I underwent a quadruple by-pass operation. Because I live on my own I had to return to Colchester for further recovery before I finally went home on the 13th of September. Andrew came to fetch me, drove me home, made me a warm drink, and saw that I was safely in bed before he went home. The hospital had set up a care package, so the next morning a carer arrived to give me a shower and to see to all I needed for the day. I had these carers for three weeks; they were very good indeed—I was thankful to have them.

The doctors who discharged me warned me it would take one year for me to fully recover. The only problem I had in those early days was a badly infected leg where the vein was removed. My doctor arranged for me to have a district nurse, she came for five weeks and eventually it healed. As I write this, in ten days time it will be eight years since I had my surgery. Since I recovered from it I have been, and am now, more well than I had been before. I am grateful to God for a new lease of life that was given to me. I am so grateful (as I wrote to the surgeons who operated on me) for the skill God has given to men and women to be able to perform such surgery. I know they are able to do greater things now.

I now live in Cambridge in a very pleasant one bedroom flat. It is because I realised I would not always be as active as I am at the moment, I made the decision to live in a warden controlled building. I have plenty of interests and lots of things to keep me occupied mentally as well as physically. When the time comes that I am not as well as I am now, I did not want to rely on friends to look after me. I have many lovely and caring friends, some of whom are more like family. I felt I needed to look to the future.

After praying about this and making various enquiries I found out about the Foundation of Edward Storey. I cannot tell you all the history, but you can look it up on the internet. Just briefly Edward Storey, a Cambridge

Captain, gentleman and bookseller, died in 1693. The charity was established in 1693. To begin with there were Almshouses for widows, some of whom were clergy widows.

Today there are forty eight sheltered flats at Storeys House on Mount Pleasant in Cambridge. There is also a care home. There is a call system in each flat in case of any emergencies.

I originally applied to the Church of England Pensions Board for sheltered accommodation. The waiting list was very long. As I waited the possibility came up of accommodation at Storeys House. I applied, came to Cambridge to have a look, then applied and went onto a waiting list. I only waited ten months and moved to Cambridge on the first of October 2008.

When I came to Cambridge for an interview I was warmly welcomed by the then Warden Jo Powell. The person in charge of the letting of the flats was able to let me see one of the flats even though it was occupied, so that I could see if it was suitable or not. I found the flats were very suitable and very nice. The building is very attractive and surrounded by gardens. I was then interviewed by Tim Burgess, who is the chief clerk to the trustees of the Edward Storey Foundation. He greeted me warmly before we sat down to discuss my application for residence.

Way before I came to Cambridge, now and again one or other of my friends would say to me "you know you really ought to write a book". It is since I came to Cambridge I began to think seriously about the possibility of writing my autobiography. When I had settled down here I went on a Creative Writing Course. It was helpful, but not really what I thought it would be; I expected the course would help me with grammar and the way I express myself. It did not do so, nevertheless I did enjoy it.

It is since I have been in Cambridge I made my second trip to South Africa which I have already written about earlier. When I saw my brother in 2002 he was not very well. He was suffering from Parkinson's disease. As we kept in touch by telephone I noticed that at times his speech sounded a bit slurred, and I would have to ask him to repeat what he had said more than once. In the end not wanting to make him feel awkward I hazarded a guess at what he was trying to say.

Three weeks before he died I had a phone call from my sister-in-law telling me Austin was in a coma. He remained in that coma and died on the 22nd of September 2009. Because of the situation and because my sister-in-law requested I did not go immediately, which I was quite willing to do, I made arrangements to be able to fly the same day when I got the news of his death. My niece phoned at 6 am British time. I went down to Thomas Cook as soon as they were open and got my ticket. In the afternoon I went by taxi to Heathrow and flew at 10.30 pm arriving at Cape Town airport at 10.30 am South African time. I am so grateful I was able to conduct a service for my brother. I returned a week later on the overnight flight from Cape Town and was back in Cambridge by midday.

I keep in contact with my sister-in-law; we phone each other once a fortnight.

It is since I moved to Cambridge that it dawned on me now is the time for me to get down to writing my life story. It has taken me a long time.

My sincere wish is that the reader will see how blessed I have been. My life may seem the kind of life many people experience. Yet, from my perspective, because I believe in the sovereignty of God, I have seen His hand in every circumstance of my life.

Wherever you are if you have read this book I pray you may be blessed by seeing what God has done in the life of one of His children.

Lightning Source UK Ltd.
Milton Keynes UK
UKOW051335220113

205187UK00004B/242/P